The International Library of Sociology

STUDIES IN CLASS STRUCTURE

Founded by KARL MANNHEIM

The International Library of Sociology

RACE, CLASS AND SOCIAL STRUCTURE
In 21 Volumes

STUDIES IN CLASS STRUCTURE

by

G. D. H. COLE

Routledge
Taylor & Francis Group

LONDON AND NEW YORK

First published in 1955 by
Routledge

Reprinted 1998, 2000 by
Routledge
2 Park Square, Milton Park, Abingdon, Oxon, OX14 4RN
711 Third Avenue, New York, NY 10017

Transferred to Digital Printing 2007

Routledge is an imprint of the Taylor & Francis Group, an informa business

First issued in paperback 2013

British Library Cataloguing in Publication Data
A CIP catalogue record for this book
is available from the British Library

Studies in Class Structure
ISBN13: 978-0-415-17638-5 (hardback)
ISBN13: 978-0-415-86342-1 (paperback)
Class, Race and Social Structure: 21 Volumes
ISBN 0-415-17826-6
The International Library of Sociology: 274 Volumes
ISBN 0-415-17838-X

Publisher's Note
The publisher has gone to great lengths to ensure the quality of this
reprint but points out that some imperfections in the original
may be apparent

Preface

O F the six studies which make up this volume, four have been published previously—two in English and two in French. (I) 'Introductory' is new. (II) 'The Influence of Technological Changes on the Development of Class Structure in the Western World' appeared in French in the Belgian periodical *Industrie* in April, 1953. It has not been published until now in English. (III) 'The Social Structure of England' appeared in two articles in *History To-day* in February and March, 1951, but has been revised for publication in this volume. (IV) 'The Conception of the Middle Classes' was originally read as a paper at the Anglo-French Historical Congress held at All Souls College, Oxford, in September, 1949, and was subsequently printed in the *British Journal of Sociology* in December, 1950. (V) 'Élites in British Society' was originally written as a contribution to a projected volume, to be published in French, dealing with the nature of élites in various European societies; but through a chapter of accidents this volume has not yet appeared, and the essay is now published for the first time. Finally, (VI) 'British Class Structure in 1951' was published in French in *Cahiers Internationaux de Sociologie* in its double issue of January to June, 1954, but is here published for the first time in English. To the editors of the periodicals concerned I make due acknowledgement for their consent to my use of these articles, which were from the first intended to form parts of a collected volume of studies.

G. D. H. COLE

All Souls College, Oxford
  April 1955.

Contents

I

Introductory

ALL the studies included in this volume are concerned with
class structure. They describe or analyse the class composition of Great Britain and of other Western Societies
from a variety of points of view, and at different stages of
development; and they are concerned largely, but by no
means exclusively, with the economic aspects of class. They
have not, however, been written on the basis of any dogmatic
theory: they do not propound any infallible criterion for
defining classes or for declaring to what class this or that
individual should be assigned. It is indeed my considered
view that no such single criterion exists and that the very
notion of class, as distinguished from that of caste or legally
recognized estate, is imprecise. Classes, at any rate as they
exist in Western countries to-day and as they have existed
in the West for a long time past, are not sharply definable
groups whose precise numbers can be determined by gathering in enough information about every individual. They
are rather aggregations of persons round a number of central
nuclei, in such a way that it can be said with confidence of
those nearer each centre that they are members of a particular class, but that those further from a centre can be
assigned to the class it represents only with increasing uncertainty. Moreover, an individual can be within the sphere
of more than one class at the same moment, so that he cannot be assigned wholly to one class; and there exist individuals who can hardly be assigned to any class, even in the
most tentative way. It does not follow, because societies
have classes within them, that every person attached to them
must be assignable to a class. Nor does it follow, though it is
often assumed, that the classes which exist in any given
society can be realistically arranged in a simple hierarchy

of superior and inferior, each class standing above or below the next. Evidently the notion of higher and lower holds an important place in that of class differentiation; but it does not stand alone. Account has also to be taken of the notion of social function—of what a person does as well as of what he is—and the relations between these two aspects are highly complex. In some societies what a person does, or is expected to do, is mainly derived from what he is, or is supposed to be. In others what he is, or is supposed to be, depends mainly on what he actually does. In a structure of closed orders, or estates, occupation is determined or limited by the personal or family status into which the individual is born. In a fully open society, if such a society existed, class would depend on occupation and achievement—unless indeed, in such a society, the notion of class ceased to be entertained at all. There are some sociologists who deny that class exists, save as a vanishing relic of the past, in the Soviet Union. There are others who deny that it exists, as a significant phenomenon, in the United States. Both these denials provoke lively counter-assertions. Communism, it is argued, far from abolishing classes, has introduced a new class structure in place of the old: American capitalism, it is argued, rests on a system of class exploitation within which wealth has largely ousted other criteria of class. It seems clear that the makers of these conflicting judgments must attach different meanings to the word. What are these meanings; and, if we can discover what they are, can we find any valid ground for regarding one meaning as correct, or as more correct than others?

The first question to ask in this context is whether there is any single criterion by which one can decide to what class a person belongs, if not in all cases, at least in enough to establish a significant standard of assignation. Unless this can be done, difficulties will evidently arise; for if account has to be taken of more than one criterion and if the different criteria indicate different answers, we shall be forced either to say simply that a person can belong to different classes according to the angle from which he is being looked at, or to find some way of assigning weights to the different criteria, in order to be able to say that so and so belongs predominantly to Class X, though he shares some characteristics of Class Y, and perhaps of Class Z as well. But how can we possibly arrive at any agreed basis for such weighting of distinct criteria? A single criterion, if a satisfactory foundation for it can be established, is obviously to be preferred. But can there be a single, generally acceptable criterion?

What sort of criterion, or criteria, are we to look for? The first problem that faces us is whether it is to be subjective or objective in its nature. One possible answer is that a person's class is simply what that person supposes it to be, or declares it to be when he is asked. But even this is not so simple as it sounds. If a random collection of persons are asked merely to what class they belong, some of them will probably give no answer at all, and will not know what answer to give. If, on the other hand, they are given a list of named classes to choose from, most of them will probably be prepared to fit themselves into one of the given categories; but it may make a considerable difference how the list is drawn up, not merely according to the number of classes that are named, but also according to the names that are used. 'Upper, middle and lower' will not produce the same distribution of answers as 'governing, middle and working', or as 'bourgeois, petit bourgeois and proletarian'; and in all probability sub-division of any main group—for example of 'middle' into 'upper middle' and 'lower middle', or of 'working' into 'skilled' and 'unskilled'—will increase the numbers of persons who assign themselves to the sub-divided category as a whole.

Apart from these difficulties, the class to which a person says that he belongs can surely not be taken as necessarily identical with the class to which he actually belongs. To assume this identity would involve regarding class as entirely a matter of subjective consciousness; but this is certainly not what most of those who have used the word either as historians or as sociologists have meant by it, even if they have recognized the presence of a subjective element. Accordingly, some sociologists have preferred, instead of asking a person to say to what class he regards himself as belonging, to ask those who are acquainted with him to state their opinions of the class to which he should be assigned. This of course means that different individuals may give different answers, and still involves the difficulty that the answers will be affected by the names given to the classes, if any list of alternatives is presented to them. Moreover, if no such list is presented, the answers will probably be given in terms of classifications too diverse to be reduced to any meaningful table of class assignments.

If these subjective methods are admitted to be unsatisfactory, can better results be got by attempting to apply an objective criterion? What form can such a criterion take? One possibility, if the necessary data can be procured, is to make income the criterion, and to arrange all income recipients in an arbitrary number of groups within certain ranges of income, irrespective of the source from which the income is derived. In that case, it would be indispensable to take as the unit of classification the family rather than the individual; but this raises difficult questions affecting the definition of the family unit and the extent to which any part of the incomes accruing to members of the family as defined should be disregarded in computing 'family income', or considered separately, and also the question whether the basis of classification should be income per family or per head. Apart from these problems it is doubtful whether anyone would be prepared to accept income as the sole criterion of class, even though it might be regarded as constituting in some cases an important factor in determining class status.

The next claimant for the place of sole, or predominant, criterion of class is occupation. This of course cannot be applied to unoccupied persons unless they have been occupied in the past; and it is not by any means satisfactory to classify retired persons in terms of the last occupation before retirement. Similar difficulties arise in connection with unemployed persons, unless they have a regular trade to which they may be expected to return, and also with children who are still at school and with young persons whose present occupation may fail to indicate their probable future and may be a misleading guide to class affiliations. Moreover, the possibility of using occupation as a clear indication of class standing depends on the existence of very elaborate occupational data; for the same occupational name, in such sources as the Population Census, may cover individuals who cannot realistically be treated as belonging to the same class group. In fact, as we shall see in one of the following essays, the occupational break-up provided by the British Census is very uneven for different occupations. The only way of handling the Census material is to take as a single unit each group that is separately designated, though this gives as a result not an assignment of each individual to the class to which he would be assigned if his case were considered separately, but only an aggregation of often arbitrary occupational units into a smaller number of class or status groups. There is in addition often a considerable uncertainty about the class or status group to which a particular occupational group can best be assigned; and, in any event, the decision how many class or status groups are to be recognized has to be arbitrarily made.

The only other criterion which could be used statistically for class-grouping of the entire population, or of most of it, would seem to be that of education in a formal sense, with school or university leaving age as the main factor to be considered. Education has clearly something to do with class; but even within this field it would be unrealistic to ignore continued part-time or spare-time education, or adult education resumed after an interval. Nor could apprenticeship and other forms of training on the job be left out of account; nor again does the time spent in one kind or another of formal education measure by itself the extent of the education actually acquired. Apart from this, it is clear that when people speak of class, whether as experts or as laymen, they hardly ever think of education as more than one factor that is relevant to settling to what class a person belongs.

We are left, then, with the conclusion that no single criterion can serve adequately as a means of assigning every person in a society to his or her appropriate class, so as to enable us to add up, even approximately, the total numbers in each class. This would not be possible even if the statistical data were greatly improved, or even if it were practicable to lay down on any scientific basis how many classes should be recognized as existing, or to agree upon their names and broad coverage in terms of such factors as income, occupation, or educational standard. At the same time, it seems to be evident that the body of statistical information likely to provide the greatest amount of indication of the class structure in any advanced society is to be found in the classification of occupations, wherever this classification is reasonably detailed—especially if its possible use for the purpose of analysis in terms of classes has been in the minds of the compilers of the statistics. There will, however, even with the best-compiled statistics, remain a large residue of persons who cannot be directly classified on this basis. Persons not gainfully occupied will have to be classified largely by assigning them to the classes to which their spouses or occupied parents belong, or by past occupation in the case of the retired; and the final result will be, not a realistic assessment of the class of each individual, but rather an allocation of occupational groups as wholes, in the hope that errors of individual classification will to some extent cancel out in the wider grouping.

In assigning particular occupations to particular classes, sociologists have sometimes attempted to use a subjective approach, by asking either a number of skilled observers or a more or less random set of persons to draw up lists of occupations and to indicate to what class they regard these occupations as belonging or to arrange them in an order of priority according to class. Certain enquiries of this sort have shown, within a single society, a substantial degree of agreement among those asked about the relative class-rating of the specified occupations, which have usually been only a limited number selected from the vast number listed in Census or other data. The preponderant opinions concerning occupational class priorities have then been used to provide a framework within which the other occupations have been fitted according to the estimators' own judgment of their relation to the specified occupations.

6

This raises a difficult problem. If a number of persons are asked, without further indication of what is wanted, to assign each of a number of occupations to one of a number of listed classes or to arrange them in an order of class priority, the answers will in all probability be related largely to the answerers' conception of the social prestige attached by common opinion to each occupation. There will be, to a substantial extent, a tacit assumption that the real criterion of class is prestige, as far as it is attached to the following of a particular occupation. But is prestige to be identified with class, or regarded as a satisfactory or sufficient criterion of it? There are in any society a number of different sources of prestige; and only some of these are related to occupation in the sense in which this term is used in the Census or in other official statistical enumerations. Occupational prestige is an important 'social fact'—to use Durkheim's phrase; but so are many other forms of prestige which have nothing to do with gainful occupation. It is surely plain common sense that, of these other forms of prestige, some have a very close connection with class, and others no connection at all. Occupational prestige clearly has a connection with class; but is this connection constant, or even nearly enough so for it to be properly used as a basis for class assignment? Finally, even if it is, can we be assured that there really is widespread agreement about the degrees of prestige to be assigned to even the most numerous occupations? For example, is the prestige scale the same in areas where the occupational structures are widely different—say, in London, in South Wales, and in a predominantly rural area such as Devonshire or Suffolk? Perhaps it is; but as far as I know, the fact of its being so has never been firmly established by adequate investigation.

Investigators who use occupation as the criterion for assignment to classes usually find the greatest difficulties confronting them, not at the top or bottom of their scale, but in the middle, and especially when they come to deal with the relative placing of skilled manual workers and of the growing bodies of routine non-manual workers in such occupations as clerical work and retail distribution. It is clearly

7

unrealistic to put all the non-manual workers of these types into a higher class than all the skilled manual workers, or vice-versa; and recognition of this usually leads to acceptance of a very large class, which may add up to more than half the total of all the occupational classes, by including both these categories. The sub-division of this large composite class into sub-classes placed in order one above another presents insuperable difficulties, even if the two main elements can be arranged separately from each other into superior and inferior groups with some degree of plausibility. Naturally so; for ordinary persons, as distinct from experts, seldom have any conception of an all-inclusive grading of occupations into higher and lower. At most they have prestige scales covering a limited number of groups; and they do not necessarily combine all the scales thay have into one. Prestige can be functional, as well as merely quantitative: in terms of prestige, or of class, as well as of the labour market, there can be 'non-competing' groups to which a common scale is not applied. Nor need every occupation— much less every individual—be classified at all in ordinary people's minds.

Nevertheless, if a single criterion is to be used, occupation is likely to be better than any other, where the purpose is to arrive at a rough estimate of the numbers of persons to be included in the various social classes. Though it cannot yield in a diversified society such as ours any accurate enumeration, and though the number of classes recognized as calling for separate treatment is bound to be arbitrary, it can throw a good deal of useful light both on class structure generally and on the internal class structure of particular industries or services and also on the changes occurring both generally and particularly from one date to another. It can be used to some purpose in attempts to study class mobility, both within a single lifetime and from one generation to the next. The existing data are indeed too scanty to yield more than a fraction of the informative conclusions that could be arrived at if better data were collected and made available; but what is available is a good deal better than what was so even a decade or two ago, and there is no reason why the improvement should not continue and be speeded up if we wish. We shall never know, objectively and beyond doubt, how many classes there are, or how many persons there are in each; for the naming and the number of the classes will always remain to some extent arbitrary and subjective, and there will always be doubts about the class to which some occupational groups can properly be assigned. But inadequate statistics may be much better than no statistics at all, provided that their shortcomings and limitations are understood.

We have, however, still to deal with not a few critics who hold that all the ways of approach so far discussed are radically wrong, and that classes either cannot properly be delimited at all, or should be so in terms of some quite different criterion. To the first of these schools of critics belong those who maintain that in the 'open' societies characteristic of advanced capitalist enterprise the conception of class has ceased to have any meaning clear or significant enough to be worth studying. When, under 'free enterprise', everyone is free to make his own place in society and there are no artificial barriers in the way of social mobility, it is argued that differences of wealth or income, or of prestige, do not constitute class differences, but only individual differences dependent on enterprise or on luck. In such societies, it is said, there can exist 'pressure groups', but not classes, because each man's status is personal and fluid. This argument seems to me to be nonsense. A class is not necessarily a body of persons cut off by impassable barriers from others: it is not necessarily hereditary or legally defined. It is not the same thing as a caste or an 'estate', though these may constitute classes. The existence in the United States of a powerful Trade Union movement of wage-earners is evidence enough of the reality of a working class in that country, even though its leaders may not base their action on a comprehensive social doctrine of 'class struggle' like that of the Marxists. American, no less than European, Trade Unions rest on the need to defend class interests and to press class claims, and have met with bitter hostility to their attempts to establish their right to act collectively on behalf of their members and to remove legal and other obstacles in the way of doing so. What those who deny the existence of classes in such a society as the United States are really denying is not class but class antagonism as a pervasive phenomenon of American society.

As against this Marxists, Syndicalists, and many other kinds of Socialists regard class antagonism as a fundamental fact of capitalist society, and see the struggle of the working class as a struggle not merely to obtain better working and living conditions but also to transform the social structure by making the workers the predominant power in society. According to Marxist doctrine class is not merely *a* social reality but *the* great social reality which transcends all others and constitutes the great moving force in history. Each stage in social development, Marxists hold, is marked by the predominance of a particular class, which constitutes itself as the ruling class; and each fresh stage brings to the front a fresh class as the chief claimant to take over rulership from the class actually in power. How, then, do Marxists define these classes, to which they assign this vital role in historical evolution? They do so in terms not of any of the criteria so far considered, but of the relation which individuals or groups stand in to the economic structure—that is, to the control and use of the powers of production. Under capitalism, they say, one set of persons owns and controls the powers of production and gives orders to another set of persons who labour at a variety of tasks under their direction and in accordance with what the ruling class conceives to be its interests. These two classes they call respectively the bourgeoisie and the proletariat; and, though they recognize the existence of other classes, they regard the struggle between these two as the only fundamentally significant factor in directing the course of modern history. Marx himself, in the Communist Manifesto, predicted that as capitalism developed further the other classes would tend to disappear, or at any rate to lose all independent significance. More and more of the persons who hold an intermediate position between capitalists and proletarians would be flung down into the proletariat as the scale of business organization grew larger and as the small independent producers were crushed out. The class of peasants would be crushed by the application of large-scale capitalist methods to agriculture, and the rural workers would thus become assimilated to the urban proletariat. Capitalism, in thus subjecting more and more of the population to its rule and discipline, could not avoid increasing the strength of the proletariat as a hostile force or prevent it from organizing for the overthrow of the capitalist order. In due course, the proletariat would become strong enough to abolish the capitalist domination and take power into its own hands.

This Marxist theory rests on a view of capitalism as tending necessarily, in consequence of technical progress, towards aggregation of the powers of production into larger masses—not only larger factory, mining, and other directly productive enterprises, but also and especially larger units of business policy-making and control through trusts, combines, and other forms of monopoly, including those of banking and finance. Marx put no stress on the possibility that this concentration of control over production might proceed side by side with a diffusion of ownership among a growing number of small share- and bond-holders who would receive among them a large proportion of the profits of production but would have for the most part practically no voice in the control of production. Nor did he attach any great significance to the tendency of large-scale enterprises to create an ever-increasing class of technicians, administrators, and supervisors in the service of capitalist business, remunerated at a variety of levels for the most part well above those of manual and clerical workers, or to the parallel tendency for the numbers of professionals outside large-scale industry to increase much faster than most other sections of the population and to constitute a growing element in the middle classes, not easily identifiable as either capitalists or proletarians. He did not of course deny the existence or growth of these groups; but he regarded the intermediate groups in industry as essentially servants of their capitalist masters and the non-industrial professions as also mainly engaged in ministering to the demands of the capitalist class. He did not see in either group the potency to set itself up as an independent force in the making of a new society, and regarded the members of both as destined either to accept the rôle of serving capitalism or to throw in their lot with the proletariat, and accept its leadership.

Of course, Marx also recognized the existence in contemporary society of aristocratic elements persisting from a pre-capitalist stage of social development. But he regarded these elements, save to the extent to which they had become fused with the bourgeoisie, as survivals from a past epoch of feudalism, and as no longer capable of playing an independent creative rôle. Similarly, he regarded the class which he called the 'petite bourgeoisie', consisting mainly of small traders and independent master-craftsmen and artisans, as an obsolescent class, destined to disappear with the further advance of large-scale enterprise and inseparably bound up with out-of-date methods of production. He saw nothing in common between the declining class of small-scale producers and the growing body of salaried technicians and managers employed in large-scale enterprise, or the growingly diversified and numerous professional groups.

Thus, for Marx, in relation to contemporary advanced societies, only two classes really counted—bourgeoisie and proletariat. The others, as far as they could be regarded as classes at all, were obsolescent. The rising intermediate groups of middle-range salaried and professional workers he refused to treat as constituting real classes because he regarded them as incapable of staking out independent claims to social mastery.

Who, in this conception of class structures, were or are the bourgeoisie—the predominant ruling class of to-day? They were essentially, in Marx's view, those who, by virtue of their ownership and control of the means of production, were able to live by exploiting the working class. But it was never made clear whether the essential characteristic of the bourgeois was ownership or control. In terms of control over the means of production it was easy enough to demonstrate the existence of a powerful tendency towards concentration in fewer hands, though there was much controversy over the question whether this tendency held good in agriculture as well as in industry, commerce, and finance. But it certainly could not be demonstrated that in general ownership as well as control was becoming concentrated: indeed, as the nineteenth century advanced, it became increasingly plain that it was not. The growing body of small capital-owners in the advanced societies dominated by joint-stock enterprise had therefore to be treated as the hangers-on of the great capitalists—the grande bourgeoisie—who in fact more and more monopolized the control. These inactive shareholders and bondholders shared with the active capitalists in the benefits of exploitation, and accordingly stood in a similar, though subordinate, relation to the powers of production, and constituted part of a single capitalist class. Over against these were ranged the productive workers, whom they exploited by paying to them in wages and salaries less than the value which their labour produced. But, according to the Marxist doctrine, not all wage- or salary-earners were producers, even if they performed essential work. Only those who actually made things, or transported them from place to place so as to add to their value, were producers. The growing hosts employed in distribution, or in commercial or service occupations, produced nothing, however necessary their labour might be. Their labour, as far as it was needed for getting commodities into the consumers' hands, constituted a necessary charge on the value of what was produced. Accordingly, these non-productive workers could not be exploited by the capitalists paying them less than the value they produced; for in Marx's view they produced nothing. Their remuneration was settled by the higgling of the labour market through their competition with the productive workers; and they had to this extent a common interest with the rest of the working class. But they were not proletarians in the full sense, because their exploitation was only indirect. Some of them would no doubt act as proletarians, because they suffered under much the same conditions of life: others, holding superior positions as managers or technicians, would tend to act with the capitalists in defence of their peculiar privileges.

We thus get a general picture of the class structure according to Marx which shows a broad division of the whole society into two contending classes, each with its lesser allies. On the one hand are the great capitalists—bankers and financiers, great industrialists and merchants, who increasingly control the use of the powers of production. Behind them are ranged the smaller fry of the same groups, who are being gradually eroded by the development of large-scale enterprise, the large body of small owners who hold shares in large-scale enterprises, and the salaried technicians and managers who hold positions of some authority in such enterprises—and also the surviving elements of the older aristocracy based mainly on landholding. Over against these classes and groups is set the main body of productive workers, depending on wages for the means of life, and employed to produce 'surplus value' for the exploiting classes; and behind these true proletarians are ranged the lower grades of non-productive workers—the black-coated proletariat—who produce no 'value' but are necessary agents in its realization. In the countryside, the large-scale farmers rank with the industrial employers, and the rural wage-labourers with the productive proletariat. Finally, between these two major groupings stands the petite bourgeoisie of small-scale traders and artisans, with the smaller farmers and the more prosperous peasants occupying an analogous position; but these intermediate groups, according to the Marxists, are in process of being crushed out by the development of modern productive methods, and are torn between their hostility to the capitalists who are threatening them with destruction and their desire to preserve themselves from becoming engulfed in the proletariat: so that, up to a point, they are prepared to support the proletariat in fighting against the capitalists, but in the last resort they tend to rally to the capitalist side in the hope of maintaining their petty property and their minor positions of privilege.

In this theory of classes the stress is laid on the relation of each class group to the powers of production, not merely as they exist, but as they are in process of becoming. The theory is dynamic and rests on a conception of destined evolution of economic forces. Under capitalism, production has been becoming more and more a 'social' process, involving both larger-scale enterprise and the collaboration of many hands in producing commodities and also a growing interdependence of one branch of production upon another. The logical conclusion of this development is complete 'socialization', which involves the unified planning and control of the entire affair. Theoretically, this could come about through the conversion of all economic enterprise into a single vast business under the control of a completely unified capitalist direction. But in practice this cannot happen because the same developments as lead to this capitalist concentration also consolidate the proletariat and endow it with the power to take the control of society out of the capitalists' hands and assume this control for itself.

How does this Marxist conception of class structure fit in with the ascertainable facts of economic evolution? Clearly, the growth of capitalist concentration is a real fact. But, though many small businesses are crushed out by the growth of large-scale enterprise, it is not a fact that small business as a category shows any sign of dying out. The small shopkeeper, as well as the peasantry, persists; and many new forms of small-scale enterprise make their appearance actually as a consequence of technical advance. Garages are established in thousands as a direct outcome of the large-scale production of motor vehicles. Small electrical businesses, from wiring contractors to wireless dealers, abound. Small builders thrive on repair and maintenance of buildings erected by major firms; the big restaurant does not cause the little restaurant or tea-shop to disappear. Instead, it is multiplied as more meals are taken away from home. No doubt, in the countries which have done away with large-scale private capitalism, the scope for small-scale business is much less than in advanced capitalist countries. But even in the Soviet Union the small enterprise has not disappeared. Where it has, moreover, it has done so not because of any necessary tendency of purely economic evolution, but because it has been deliberately displaced as a matter of policy by the victorious proletarian revolution.

One highly significant effect of Marxist class theory has been to identify the cause of the proletariat with the advance of large-scale production. The wage-workers in large-scale industry have been regarded as the protagonists in the struggle for the conquest of power; and all other elements have been undervalued, or even denied any creative rôle. The great significance of the Communist Revolution in China is that it was achieved by recognizing the creative force of the peasants and making the reform of the land system in the peasants' interests the main means of attracting popular support. Without this the Revolution could hardly have been victorious in face of the backwardness of Chinese industry. No doubt, the victors are now straining every nerve to force the pace of industrial development, without which China cannot hope to assume a leading place in the world economy. But the Chinese show at present no signs of following the Russian example of enforced collectivization of agriculture. This, indeed, in the extreme form which it took in Russia, was mainly the outcome of a dogmatic belief that large-scale production must be superior to small-scale and that the Revolution could not maintain itself unless the condition and mental outlook of the peasants could be assimilated to those of the workers in large-scale industry. The Chinese, if they continue to avoid this form of megalomania, have the chance to build their new economic order with much less cost in human suffering and with much less dictatorial force than have gone into the building of the Soviet Union under Stalinist control.

In Marxist theory the class is regarded, not merely as a collection of persons having a common status and relation to the powers of production, but as a reality somehow transcending the individuals who make it up. This view of class as a superior reality is derived mainly from the Hegelian element in Marx's social philosophy. Marx saw capitalism as a force acting through modern technology to depersonalize the individual worker and reduce him to the rôle of a ' detail-labourer', of a mere unit in a mass of 'abstract human labour'; and, far from setting himself in opposition to this tendency, Marx thought of it as an essential part of the process of 'socialization'. Consequently, he laid his entire emphasis on the victory of the proletariat as a class, and conceived of emancipation as meaning the transference of power to the class as a whole, rather than to the individuals included in it. This is the basis of the doctrine which treats the Communist Party as the sole legitimate representative of the working class and insists on complete unity of action and the extermination of all forms of articulated dissent. It provides the justification for what is called 'democratic centralism' and for one-party government. Marxists who hold this creed, when they have achieved power, naturally set out to bring the social structure into conformity with it. But, as they cannot dispense with leadership or with individuality in either political or economic affairs, they are compelled to establish new forms of differentiation which can be reconciled with their view of the nature of class. Stakhanovism is an obvious instance. The Stakhanovite is allowed and encouraged to earn an income far above that of his fellow-workers; but this, it is argued, does not constitute any sort of class difference because his relation to the powers of production remains the same as theirs. Thus, in the Russian view, a high degree of economic inequality does not involve class antagonism where it rests on difference of productive service, but only where it arises out of a different relation—for example, out of the possession of property in the means of production.

In contrast to the Russian endeavour to assimilate almost everybody to the status of a wage-worker, labouring for the 'collective' instead of the capitalist, upholders of private enterprise often nowadays put forward the ideal of a 'property-owning democracy', in which every citizen would own some share in the means of production. They point to the considerable diffusion of small shareholding in the United States and in other advanced countries, and point out that the increasing divorce between ownership and control in large-scale enterprise makes it possible to get the technical benefits of concentration without the monopoly of ownership by a narrow group; and they also in many cases advocate the development of profit-sharing in order to make the employed workers sharers in the profits of enterprise. They do not as a rule suggest that either the smaller shareholders or the employed workers can as such secure any substantial control over large-scale business; but they usually argue that the entire population have, as consumers, the final control in their hands through their power to transfer their custom unless they find they are getting a fair deal. Consumption, it is said, binds all classes and groups together in a common interest in getting what they want at a fair price: there are no sharply marked-off classes of consumers because, to a substantial extent, the rich and the poor consume the same things, though in different amounts and often in different qualities. The existence of vast Consumers' Co-operative movements in many countries clearly makes against the view that working-class consumers have no distinct interests of their own. It is nevertheless true that consumers are marked off by class differences a good deal less sharply than producers, and that the way in which incomes are procured gives a better clue than their amount to the class affiliation of the recipients.

Even, however, if the *form* of income received is accepted as the least misleading single criterion of class, it must be recognized that this criterion does not yield, in the most advanced capitalist societies, conclusions which bear out Marx's expectations of increasing polarization. Such societies indeed include a number of very rich and very poor individuals and households; but it is by no means the case that the intermediate income groups are decreasing in relative size. On the contrary, they have increased, and are increasing. Marxists may answer that this is irrelevant, because they are defining classes not in terms of size of income, but in terms of their relation to the productive system. But it is no less evident that these relations, far from being simplified into a sharper difference between capitalists and exploited persons, tend on the whole to become more differentiated. As compared with the situation when Marx surveyed it, the proportion of occupied persons engaged in providing physical commodities has fallen off and the proportion engaged in transporting them, after increasing, has begun again to decline in the more advanced societies, whereas the proportion engaged in services—sometimes called 'tertiary industry'—has increased despite a large decline in that of private domestic servants. The central proletariat of manual-working 'producers' does not constitute a majority in the most advanced countries, even if the agricultural wage-workers are counted in. In Great Britain in 1951, as we shall see in a subsequent essay, out of each hundred occupied heads of households enumerated in the Census, manual workers of all types, including agricultural workers and soldiers, sailors and airmen, accounted for 61·6, and workers engaged in personal services for 4·1. Clerical workers and shop assistants together accounted for 8·2, and foremen and lesser supervisors for 4. Shopkeepers and small employers accounted for 4·9, farmers for 2·7. Managerial, administrative and professional workers, including medium and large employers, accounted for 21·1, out of whom 3·3 were assigned by the Census to a higher and 18·8 to a lower sub-group. These proportions exclude the unoccupied and the retired, and include only heads of households; and they do not separate manual workers employed in production from those in other types of work. An alternative classification covering all occupied and retired males, but excluding females, groups the whole occupied population into five 'social classes', each scheduled occupation being treated as a single unit and assigned wholly to one class. This puts 52·5 per cent of the total into the third class, which is made up of skilled workers, including blackcoats and supervisors as well as manual workers. Above this are 3·3 per cent in the top and 14·8 per cent in the second class. Below are 16·4 per cent in the fourth class, made up of persons regarded as semi-skilled, and 13 per cent in the bottom class of unskilled workers. The three classes nearest the bottom thus together constitute 81·9 per cent of the total, but this figure includes the bulk of the non-manual workers, among them the supervisors as well as many of the lesser professional workers. Such classifications, as we have seen, are bound to be to a large extent arbitrary. The essay in which the Census data are studied in greater detail attempts to elucidate their meaning as far as these data allow. In general what emerges is that though the manual workers of all types considerably outnumber all the rest, the producers, as defined by Marx, do not. This is borne out by the analysis of total man-power, including all classes, published monthly in the official *Digest of Statistics*. According to this *Digest*, in July 1954, out of a total working population of 23,578,000, those engaged in manufacturing industries numbered 9,028,000. Agriculture, forestry and fishing accounted for 1,079,000, mining and quarrying for 867,000, building and contracting for 1,422,000, the main public utility services for 375,000, and transport and communication for 1,707,000. The total of 14,478,000 makes up 61·5 per cent of the entire occupied population; but it includes all the employers, managers, technicians, supervisors and other blackcoated workers attached to these industrial groups. The remainder of the working population is made up of 838,000 in the armed forces, 2,712,000 in the distributive trades, and 5,300,000 in professional, financial and other services, including public administration. There is an unanalysed residue of 228,000 unemployed persons.

These 14½ million persons engaged in production and transport include at least 10 per cent who are either em-ployers or managers, or self-employed, or are classified in the Census on other grounds as belonging to the first or the second 'social' class. If the total is reduced to exclude these groups, the number left is roughly 13 million out of 23½ million—still a majority. But this majority still includes the clerical and routine administrative workers and the super-visory grades, which may well account for another 10 per cent. To exclude these would reduce the productive workers to roughly 11½ millions, or roughly to 50 per cent of the total occupied population. Thus, in Great Britain to-day, roughly one occupied person out of two is a producer of surplus value, and can be assigned to the proletariat properly so called. I do not, of course, accept as valid this Marxist distinction between producers and non-producers of value: I am only pointing out to what conclusion it leads. Nor am I suggesting that Marxists in practice limit their conception of the proletariat to ' productive' workers. Clearly, they do not, but include in it wage- and salary-earners employed in many non-productive occupations. They do, however, tend to regard the wage-earning value-producers, as defined by Marx, as forming the central core of the proletariat, and to exclude most of those engaged in agricultural occupations from this central core, on which the creative force of the proletarian class and its potential allies must fundamentally depend. This central part of the proletariat nowhere constitutes a majority of the occupied population—not even in Great Britain, where agriculture occupies too small a proportion greatly to affect the balance. It does, however, constitute, in the most advanced countries, the largest single element—if it can be regarded as a single element. But can it? In Great Britain, yes, to a considerable extent; but much less so in countries where the working force is made up of a mixture of racial groups, differing widely in occupational status and in earning power. In South Africa, white, black, and coloured workers certainly do not constitute at present an unified proletarian class; and in the United States recent immigrants, as well as negroes, make up an imperfectly assimilated element.

Of course, in those countries in which Communist Revolutions have actually occurred there has been no question of the proletariat constituting more than a minority of the population. Both Russia and China were overwhelmingly peasant countries when their respective Revolutions took place; and neither had more than a small body of industrial workers employed in large-scale production. Russia's industrial sector did indeed include a few very large and technically advanced establishments in the heavy industries; and the workers from these and other largish factories and from mines and oil-wells played a key part in making the Revolution and in consolidating the power of the new régime. But these elements formed only a very small part of the occupied population; and the Revolution could hardly have established itself unless it had been able to carry a large fraction of the peasants and small-scale producers along with it. It was indispensable for the Bolsheviks, who could not hope for united peasant support, to drive a wedge between the more prosperous and the poorer peasants and to attach the latter to the Revolution by giving them land. The Stolypin régime set up after the defeat of the earlier Revolution of 1905 had been based, in the countryside, on the development of a relatively prosperous upper peasantry capable of applying improved methods of cultivation and marketing, in the hope of using this group as an anti-revolutionary force. The Bolsheviks, under Lenin's guidance, took the side of the poor peasants against the kulaks in the processes of land distribution which followed the Revolution. They thus won a following in the rural areas at the expense of their rivals, the Social Revolutionaries, who sought to represent the peasant class as a whole. Only when the new régime had consolidated its strength and seemed proof against immediate counter-revolution or serious foreign intervention did Lenin's successors venture to attempt mass-collectivization in the villages, in the hope of assimilating the peasant way of life to that of the industrial workers—a policy which was ultimately successful, though its immediate cost in human suffering and economic loss was prodigiously high. In the meantime the electoral system was weighted heavily in favour of the towns against the rural areas; and although the political structure was described as a dictatorship of workers and peasants, there was never any doubt that the industrial workers were meant to be the predominant partners, despite their numerical inferiority.

In China the workers in large-scale industry formed an even smaller section of the population than in Russia, and were largely concentrated in Manchuria and Shanghai. The Chinese Revolution could not be based upon these elements with any hope of success. Mao and his followers won their victory by building directly on peasant support; and because of this, the Chinese peasant counts for much more than did the Russian peasant in the control of the new order. The Chinese Communists are of course now hard at work building up large-scale industry, and therewith creating an industrial proletariat over the country as a whole. But they have shown the practicability, where the nationalistic impulse to freedom from foreign control can be enlisted on the side of the Revolution, of winning power with the peasantry rather than the industrial workers acting as the spearhead of the movement, and have thus provided a revolutionary model much more applicable than the Russian to conditions in many other economically backward areas.

The paradox has been widely noted that the great Revolutions professedly based on Marxist principles have occurred not in the countries of advanced capitalist enterprise, but rather in economically undeveloped countries. This would indeed be surprising if Marx's forecasts of the course of capitalist development and of the coming changes in class structure under capitalism had been even approximately correct. If, in the advanced countries, the lot of the proletariat had been 'increasing poverty', and if the members of the intermediate class groups had been flung down into the proletariat so as to share this poverty, revolution would in all probability have been the outcome. But in fact, from the middle of the nineteenth century onwards—that is, from the period when Marx formulated his social doctrine—the standards of living for the main body of the workers rose almost continuously, and at the same time the numbers of persons in the intermediate income groups, and especially in the professions, rose much faster than total population and were largely recruited from the class below them. These developments, even though their reality was often denied, diverted an increasing proportion of working-class opinion from revolutionary to reformist attitudes and thus deprived the revolutionary movement of much of its potential leadership. On the other hand, in the countries which lagged behind in economic and social development, the Marxist analysis continued to fit the situation a good deal better, or at any rate seemed more plausible because of its revolutionary appeal.

Marx's prophecy of 'increasing misery' and class polarization in the capitalist countries rested largely on his belief that capitalism, because of its inherent 'contradictions', was destined to be plunged into recurrent crises of ever-increasing severity and amplitude. But in fact there was no capitalist crisis comparable in severity with that of the Hungry Forties until the world depression which reached its nadir in 1932. Then indeed the Marxists took heart and emphatically re-asserted their prophecies of impending capitalist collapse. But the depression of the 1930s, devastating though it was, did not destroy capitalism. It brought Hitler to power in Germany and thus sowed the seeds of the second world war; but in the United States its effect was to enforce the intro-duction of structural reforms under the New Deal, and to strengthen the Trade Unions, not as a revolutionary but as an essentially reformist force. Moreover, in both America and Europe, it caused the 'Keynesian' revolution in economic doctrines, which armed the capitalist countries with greatly improved weapons for maintaining employment and thus taking the edge off social discontent. It needs a rash man now to prophesy that capitalism is destined speedily to collapse because of its inherent contradictions, or that, in the ad-vanced capitalist countries, social revolution is to be expected round the next corner.

I have discussed the Marxian aspects of class theory and action at some length in this introductory essay ; but in this volume as a whole the emphasis is rather on description and analysis of classes as they are than on the morals to be drawn in respect of action. Of the five studies contained in it, three are mainly historical—two of them international and one relating entirely to Great Britain. The two remain-ing studies deal with the class structure of contemporary British society. One of these is an attempt to extract what can be extracted about class structure from the material supplied by the Census of 1951, or rather from the pre-liminary reports so far published. The other is a non-statistical study, prepared originally for an international symposium, of the nature of what are called élites in the British social structure of the present day. Élites, of course, are not classes, though they have in some cases a class basis. Any essay upon them is bound to be largely a matter of opinion rather than of agreed fact; and I have made my own approach to the question without any attempt to fit it into Pareto's conception or to that of any other thinker who has made use of the notion. Élites, as I understand the word, are those individuals or groups of individuals who in fact play in a society, or in any significant part of a society, a key rôle in influencing attitudes and thus affecting policy. I have not attempted in my essay to deal with all kinds of élites: I have for example said nothing of them in relation to the arts, in which they play a highly significant rôle. My essay is limited to élites in the politico-economic field, or in fields closely connected with it, because it is there such competence as I have to discuss the subject lies.

I make no pretence that these essays constitute a 'book', in the sense of a fully unified whole. They have been written, except this introductory study, for particular occasions and, in four cases out of five, at someone's particular request. I had in mind at one time the possibility of using some of the material they embody in a more systematic treatment; but I see no chance of being able to find time for this, and I think, in view of the paucity of published writing about the whole subject, they are worth publishing as they are, with only such unity of treatment as comes of their being all the product of the same author and the outcome of much thought and university teaching over a number of years.

II

The Influence of Technological Changes on the Development of Class Structure in Western Europe [1]

UP to a point, the influence exercised by the growth of economic technology on the class structure of Western society is too evident and too indisputable in its nature for more than the merest summary to be needed. Everywhere in the older countries—and in most of the newer as well—it has manifested itself in a fall in the proportion of the population living by work on the land, in a growth of towns and concentrated industrial settlements, and in the development, sooner or later, of some sort of organized working-class movement, based mainly on the industrial workers. It has further revealed itself as a force making, in the more highly developed countries in their more recent stages of growth, for a decline in the proportion of the population living by direct production, either agricultural or industrial, and for a rapid growth of the numbers engaged in what are now often called 'tertiary industries'—that is to say, in service occupations, such as commerce, finance, public administration in all its branches, and the professions. At this late stage of technological development, the proportion of workers engaged in transport, which rose rapidly at earlier stages, has tended to become more nearly constant, or even to fall, whereas the proportion of 'white-collar' workers has continued to rise at an ever-increasing rate.

Of course, these are only broad generalizations, and there is no standard pattern for the distribution of man-power in a country at a particular point in the growth of its technological knowledge and equipment. A great deal depends on

[1] Reprinted from *Industrie*, 23 December, 1952.

the size of the country in relation to its population, on the nature and extent of its mineral resources, on its geographical situation and character, and on many other factors which make the influence of technology act upon it in a peculiar way. Nevertheless, the broad generalization stands. As a country begins to apply technological discoveries to the arts of production, its towns grow in population faster than its rural areas, its industrial output rises faster than the output of its agriculture, and before long it employs an increasing proportion of its man-power in transport and commerce, including distribution. Then, later as a rule, the growth of its transport slows down relatively to the whole, while the growth of 'tertiary' employments proceeds faster than ever.

These are mere commonplaces for the economic historian. But there are other factors which are less widely appreciated, and it is to these that I wish to draw attention in the present study.

Take first the growth of manufacturing industry, with which those who write about the Industrial Revolution usually begin because it was in this field, and especially in the textile industries, that technology made in the early stages its most spectacular advance. There are two things that particularly call for notice in the early growth of the factory system in textiles in the late eighteenth and early nineteenth centuries. In the first place, the pioneering textile factories using power were manned very largely by women and children, who replaced for the most part not skilled craftsmen but other women and children who had worked at home producing the same kind of product—spun yarn— without the aid of power. Weaving passed over considerably later than spinning to the factory system, and plain weaving well ahead of fancy weaving; and *plain* weaving under the domestic system, though a male trade, was no more than semi-skilled. Thus, it was some time before the textile revolution effectively displaced any considerable skilled craft (woolcombing was the first large-scale example); and before this had occurred the new, highly skilled craft of mule-spinning had been brought into existence by the advent of the power-driven machine. Moreover, in weaving, though

27

the factory system destroyed the handloom weavers, causing great and prolonged suffering in the process, the new craft of power-loom weaving was fully as skilled (though open to women) as the handicraft which it destroyed, save perhaps in the very highest ranges. There was in effect no *net* reduction in the demand for skill—only a change in its character. What the change did destroy was, first, a great deal of family employment in the home, or in small workshops attached to it, and, secondly, the special skill of weaving on the handloom. As against this, it created new skilled crafts, mule-spinning, power-loom weaving, machine woolcombing, and a number of others which later provided the basis for powerful craftsmen's trade unions.

Secondly, the revolution in the textile industries did not in its earlier phases make for urban concentration in any direct way. On the contrary, its dependence on water-power led the new factory employers of necessity to build their factories where they could find a supply of water to drive their wheels; and this meant, in most cases, building in the country beside a stream which was not suitable, or not needed, for transport. Consequently, many factories were built well away from existing towns, though often not far away; and then towns or industrial villages grew up round the factories, and gradually these settlements either turned into large towns or became part of neighbouring older towns as the space between them and the old town was filled up by houses or by further factories, great or small. This, however, for the most part did not and could not occur until water-power had been largely replaced by steam-power. The advent of steam as the main motive force emancipated the manufacturer, save in certain industries which required large and continuous supplies of water, from the need to locate his factory beside a stream. As soon as this necessity was removed, it became preferable in most cases to build the new factories in towns where a supply of workers could be attracted more easily than where the employer had to incur the cost of housing his workers and providing for most of their needs in order to get the labour he required. Thus, the change from water-driven to coal-driven machinery was the principal factor in accelerating urban concentration; and it also exercised a very great influence on the nature of the relation between employer and worker.

Under the water-power system paternalism flourished, or at all events the employer was endowed, almost of necessity, with an immense power over the lives of the workers, outside as well as within the hours of work. He had also to employ his workers much more regularly and over much longer periods, for fear of not being able to replace them; and he often employed all the members of the family. When industry became more closely urbanized the separate working forces attached to particular factories became more and more merged into a general labour force in the area—a force which could shift more easily from one employer to another, but also a force for which no single employer needed to feel a particular responsibility. Paternalism, in its good as well as in its bad aspects, tended to decay: the 'cash nexus' denounced by Thomas Carlyle became the preponderant characteristic of the relation between employer and worker, and this change fostered the growth both of trade unions and of employers' combinations against them.

Naturally, these forces acted differently, and with differing strength, from country to country. There survived, and survive to-day, in all highly industrialized countries, small-town factories which dominate the local prospects of employment and often preserve some paternalistic character. Such factories are common in small French towns and, I think, in parts of Germany. There are also, in smaller numbers, great factories which dominate larger towns, or have even created towns round them, particularly in the heavy industries; and examples of both kinds are naturally more frequent in countries of wide area in relation to population, and of the former in countries where industrialism has been superimposed on a previous pattern of numerous small towns serving as centres for surrounding primarily agricultural districts. But in general the tendency has been for the industrial town to become the location of a number of independent factories, and for the greater part of the local labour force to become a general supply of man-power on which employers draw as they need it, without attaching to themselves permanently more than a nucleus of skilled workers, and in particular without employing whole families in a single establishment.

I have been speaking so far mainly, though not exclusively, of the textile industries, which took the lead in the early development of factory production, and drew the largest numbers of workers away from the land or from the older skills. In mining and, to a large extent, in the heavy industries also, conditions affecting location have been necessarily different. Mining has to settle where the ores are to be found; and metal manufacture has its location largely determined by the costs of transporting its materials and fuel. In the nineteenth century, the heavy metal industries everywhere settled in close proximity to deposits of coal or iron, or preferably both. Where both could not be had close by, fuel economy gradually altered the economy of location, which varies with the relative amounts of materials and fuels needed; and, as industries of this type came to depend increasingly on sea-borne imports, proximity to ports became an increasingly important factor. Coal-mining never became urbanized except by accident—where a coalfield underlay or was close by a town which was, or became, a centre of other industries. Metal manufacture did become urbanized to a greater extent, but was for the most part late in doing so, whereas the finishing branches of the metal industries and the main branches of engineering settled largely in towns containing a number of establishments. The basic branches of iron- and steel-making kept for a long time, and to some extent still keep, a character and a way of life more closely akin to the industrial villages of coal-mining than to the general run of manufacturing towns. This has had important effects on class sentiment and on labour relations, because of the relative isolation of their workers from workers in other occupations and of the consequent engagements of whole families—indeed, usually of most families—in a single industry. Such areas have, of course, been notable also in most cases for the relative scarcity of opportunities for women's employment, at any rate since women have ceased in the more advanced countries to be employed in the heavier types of manual work.

In the areas where mining developed, and commonly heavy industry with it, the growth of these types of production was fully as important in the long run as that of lighter manufacturing; but it was less noticed in the earlier stages. This was so partly because for a long time miners and iron-workers continued to be thought of by most people as simply labourers, and were in fact drawn largely from the ranks of agricultural workers, whereas the factories were observed to be replacing old domestic trades and agglomerating their workers into towns. It was also because the factories employed much greater numbers of women, and also of town children whose sufferings attracted much more attention from philanthropists than those of the children in the much less visited mines and ironworks. Miners and heavy metal-workers were often looked on as a race of savages, set apart from the rest of society, and too uncouth to be touched by reforming zeal. Legislation for the protection of women and children began in respect of factories long before it reached the mines or the basic manufactures of metal; and the social effects of this retardation remain to some extent even to-day.

The second main phase of the Industrial Revolution—after the opening phases in textiles, mining, and metal manufacture—had three main aspects. These were the rapid growth of railway transport and of shipbuilding, the application of scientific methods to the production of machines, and the rapid development of banking and of industrial investment. Railway building, indeed, occupied a key position in all these fields; for, in addition to the large social effects of the actual building of the railroads, the need for improved locomotives greatly stimulated scientific engineering and precision methods in making machine components, and the large masses of capital needed for railway enterprise had marked effects both on banking and on the forms of business structure. The locomotive (and also the marine engine) designers led the way in skilled machine construction, and helped the advance of machine-making in many other fields; and the railway promoters were foremost in

31

devising new ways of gathering in capital from large numbers of investors, great and small, and thus opened the road for the general acceptance of the joint stock structure and of limited liability as the normal way of organizing large-scale enterprise.

The railways were, moreover, a powerful influence in breaking up local isolation, not only on account of the greater ease of movement which resulted from them, but also because the actual process of building them brought thousands of strangers into country areas, and often led to the establishment of industries for servicing them in the countries where they were built. Not only in Great Britain, but in many parts of the world, the 'navvy' became a familiar social figure, and many thousands of workers were drawn from the land into industry through taking jobs in railway construction and maintenance.

The railways, again, provided in Great Britain and to a smaller extent in many other countries the first kind of joint stock investment to be widely held by small investors. Moreover, where their capital was to a considerable extent raised locally in the areas in which they were being built, they did a great deal to diffuse the idea of joint stock enterprise outside financial and big business circles. This was less the case where the railways were largely built by foreign (usually British) companies or contractors, and where state guarantees or actual state investments played an important part. But almost everywhere the railway company helped to prepare the way for the *société anonyme* in other types of business, and especially in manufacture.

The rôle of banking differed more widely from country to country. The investment bank was foremost where there was the greatest difficulty in raising industrial capital by direct appeals to the public—that is, largely, where there was less free money in the hands of persons who did not wish to use it themselves in business enterprise. This was the position in most of the countries of western continental Europe. In Great Britain, because of the early development of an extensive middle class with spare money to invest, banking developed chiefly as deposit banking, and the specialized investment banks and agencies found their main fields of activity overseas, or rather in organizing foreign lending. With the development of deposit banking went the widespread substitution of cheques for currency in personal as well as in business transactions, and a greater readiness to hold liquid resources in bank deposits rather than in cash or bullion, with marked effects in accelerating the rate of monetary circulation and thus in part offsetting the consequences of scarcity of gold.

These three interrelated aspects of the Industrial Revolution in its second phase all connoted increased mobility—of human beings and of merchandise, of money both for current spending and for investment, and of capital equipment. They also created new skills—those of the engine-builder and the engine-driver, of the signalman and the civil engineer, of the banker and company promoter, and of the managers and under-managers and technicians in many forms of enterprise. At the same time the technical changes destroyed old manual skills and in many occupations drove particular kinds of small employer to the wall; but they created more than enough new skills to replace those they did away with, and, though the proportion of workers employed in large concerns increased steadily, there continued to be enough openings for new small-scale business, especially in making components for larger firms or in shopkeeping, for the total decline in the proportion of small businesses to be much slower than it was often supposed to be. Moreover, in some industries the domestic craftsmen put up a long fight against the factory system, not only in such special cases of high skill as that of the Jura watchmakers, but also in less skilled occupations in which the economies of large-scale production were not very great, as in many branches of the clothing industry. Often, indeed, the worst conditions prevailed in industries in which the large-scale merchant dealt with petty entrepreneurs or subcontractors, who in turn either conducted small workshops or bought the product of domestic labour, or gave the materials out to be processed in the workers' homes for a highly competitive piecework price. France and Belgium

33

both furnished many examples of this type of employment—even more than Great Britain, where it was largely confined to the tailoring and kindred trades and to some minor branches of manufacture. Paris *émeutisme* seems to have derived a good deal of its motive power from the workers employed under these highly objectionable conditions; and I think there were analogues in Belgian social history.

Sweated labour, then, constituted a growing problem, side by side with the advance of large-scale production, which in general afforded rather higher standards. But if there was a deeply-rooted social problem of the submerged tenth, this by no means connoted, as the *Communist Manifesto* of 1848 made out, any general tendency towards 'increasing misery' or towards the reduction of the working classes to a 'homogeneous mass of abstract labour-power'. Far from it: the skilled manual labour class grew larger, relatively as well as absolutely; and any relative decline in the position of small employers and independent workers was much more than offset by increases in the supervisory and managerial personnel of large-scale industry and by the very rapid growth of the professions—including the minor professions which achieved recognition in steadily increasing numbers. A rise in the status as well as in the numbers of the professions was indeed a very marked feature of the period. Apothecaries became doctors; school teachers, recruited largely from working-class families, acquired professional standing; and new technological professions came into existence at a great rate. Civil engineers were supplemented by gas, water, mechanical, sanitary, mining, and a host of other specialist engineering professions; and accountants, actuaries, quantity surveyors, and many other professions giving specialist services to business achieved an organized and socially recognized status.

All this occurred before the modern age of mass-production set in, and before electricity and chemistry—much more, before physics—had established their full status in the field of production. The outstanding feature of the third phase of the Industrial Revolution, which had begun well before the first world war, was the advent of forms of mass-production and mechanization which, on the one hand, greatly reduced the demand for heavy, unskilled manual labour and on the other broke down and mechanized many types of work previously done by skilled craftsmen into operations calling for no more than a relatively simple kind of dexterity which could be quickly learned and fairly easily transferred from one machine to another. In the manufacturing industry, the proportion of skilled craftsmen began to fall; but the craftsmen who survived were often required to possess higher skill, and there were many new posts for draughtsmen, toolroom craftsmen and machine-technicians, rate-fixers, and minor administrators, so that the roads to promotion were not closed to the better products of the developing services of technical and other vocational education. There was, however, a decline in the relative status of the ordinary skilled worker, measured in part by a decrease in wage-differentials which was greatly accentuated during the period of rising prices that ended in 1920 and was carried still further during the second world war.

Already, during this third phase, a gulf had opened up between the new industries, which depended directly on the ability to apply scientific knowledge, and the older industries which were still largely dominated by rule of thumb. Engineering, metallurgy, and chemicals—soon joined by electrical engineering—were industries which depended on the services of highly trained technicians, capable of understanding and applying scientific discoveries; whereas most of the older industries were managed by men who, even if they knew how to employ up-to-date machines, were unable to read scientific papers or to make good use of the services of scientists or technologists of the higher rank. To-day, in the fourth phase of the Industrial Revolution, this difference between industries still largely remains; but it is coming to be more and more blurred by the development of synthetic materials and by the manifold ramifications of modern physics and chemical engineering. These developments bring the academic scientists much closer to industry: they make scientific research and the testing out of its results on a commercial scale essential links in the chain of efficient

35

production in more and more industries; and they create the need, not only for many more scientists and higher technologists, but also for a host of trained persons to assist them both in the research station and in the factory.

All this means that, instead of an undifferentiated proletariat plunged into 'increasing misery', modern industry is dispensing with the 'bottom dogs' who used to do the unskilled, unpleasing, heavy labour, and is creating, on the one hand, a great body of semi-skilled or merely dexterous machine-minders, fairly easily transferable from job to job, and, on the other, an increasingly differentiated upperworking, or lower-middle, class composed of a mixture of highly skilled manual precision workers and of 'whitecollar' workers possessing specialized technical or administrative qualifications. This, of course, goes with a parallel transformation in the field of both general and technical education—a raising of minimum standards accompanying a higher school-leaving age and better equipped schools and teachers (apart from the temporary setbacks resulting from war), and at the same time a rapid growth of opportunities to acquire technical qualifications of various kinds for a sufficient minority to meet the expanding needs of modern productive methods.

It is highly significant that these characteristics of modern industrialism appear equally in the capitalistic United States and in the Communist Soviet Union—and indeed, more in these two countries than in either Great Britain or most parts of continental Western Europe. Technological conditions everywhere deeply influence, if they do not fully determine, the educational pattern; and the pattern of education reacts on the pattern of class behaviour and class relations.

There are some who see in these developments the advent of a new class system, resting on what they call the 'managerial revolution'. But this is, I think, a misleading view of the situation. The essence of the class systems of the past has been, not indeed that they were closed—for that none has ever been for long, in practice, however much some may have tried to close the doors on class mobility—but that the boundaries of each class were, for the most part, sharply defined. There were nobles and not-nobles, gentle folk and common persons, professional men and merely tolerated lesser practitioners, craftsmen and labourers, each group with its fairly definite social status in relation to others. But to-day, even if the applied scientists, the technologists, and the higher administrators form in effect a governing industrial *élite*, they constitute nevertheless a most indefinite group, in no respect clearly marked off from those outside the inner circle of power. It is true that there is in most countries a considerable hereditary element, both because there are still many inherited opportunities in family business and because successful parents transmit the advantages of higher education to their children. But though it remains harder for the clever children of poor than of well-to-do parents to rise in the social scale, there is no absolute exclusion, and the gates are continually pushed a little further open by the pressure from those outside. The hereditary element in social status and achievement has lost a great deal of ground, even in the older countries; and the lesser professionals and technicians form a new bridge between the higher and lower classes not less than the rising small employers did in the early phases of the Industrial Revolution.

I have been concerned in this study not to point morals, but to choose for presentation salient facts and trends. The four phases into which I have divided the process of technological change since the latter years of the eighteenth century are of course to some extent arbitrary: it would be equally possible to break up the whole process into a different number of epochs. The four I have selected have, however, been designed for the special purpose of bringing out the relations between technical changes and the class structures of the societies in which they occur. Thus, I have tried to show that what I have called the first phase, marked above all by the rapid growth of factory production with the aid of power-driven machines, created an industrial proletariat which was not indeed absolutely poorer than its predecessors who worked in their homes or in small workshops usually without power, but was more conspicuous because of its concentration, more capable of united action, and, as towns grew, subjected to increasingly evil environmental conditions with which it was nobody's recognized responsibility to cope. At this stage, it did look very much as if the Industrial Revolution were bringing about a mass-condition of 'increasing misery', and as if there were a tendency, likely to gain further force, towards the fusion of the working class into the mass of 'abstract, undifferentiated labour power' of which Marx wrote in his economic books and pamphlets. But, even at this stage, new skills were actually being born out of the power-driven machine—cotton spinning, metal-smelting, improved coal-hewing, and many more—and there was also beginning that development of the professions— country doctors, local attorneys, nonconformist ministers, school-teachers, and others—which was to gain added momentum with every increase in the total production of wealth and in the numbers of the employing, trading, and investing classes.

In the second phase, which set in with the advent of railways and steamships and the development of precision engineering (Whitworth's gauges and the improvement of the lathe in particular), the creation of new skills based on the machine was greatly extended and speeded up, and a new class of skilled manual workers gradually became powerful enough to improve its wages and working conditions and to achieve a recognized status. At this stage wage-differentials increased; and the unskilled part of the labour force fell behind. Cheap labour was drawn into the towns from the countryside, especially for railway building and subsequently railway operation; and these recruits mingled with the unskilled of the towns to form a proletariat which lacked leadership because the skilled workers, who alone could have led it, were too much occupied with establishing and improving their own position. At the same time, side by side with an accelerated increase in the professions, there was a very rapid development of commerce, distribution, and finance, creating new opportunities for the achievement of a status of social superiority at a wide variety of levels; and there was also a growth of big business concerns needing

large masses of capital, and at the same time a wider diffusion of investment, made possible by the spread of joint
stock enterprise from railways to an ever-increasing number
of types of manufacturing industry.

In the third phase, characterized by the growing application of science, especially in metallurgy and in the various
branches of engineering—and also on a smaller scale in the
chemical industries—the economies of large-scale production
greatly increased, and there began to emerge a new structure
of the labour force, with relatively fewer unskilled heavy
jobs, many more semi-skilled jobs of machine-minding calling
for dexterity rather than real craftsmanship, and higher
requirements of skill from a smaller proportion of the total
labour force. With these changes went, in the industries that
developed the fastest, a rise in the importance of, and
demand for, technicians and managerial workers, including
accountants and other financial executants, skilled buyers
and salesmen, and a whole army of clerks and presently
typists—these last being found in rapidly increasing numbers
among girls who in most cases left their jobs when they
married. The upshot was a much greater differentiation
within the classes of employed persons, and a blurring of
the lines of division between wage- and salary-earners, and
therewith between the 'workers' and the 'lower middle
class'. In this same phase, investment became still further
diffused, and small investments became much more important among the better paid manual workers, especially in
those countries in which Consumers' Co-operation achieved
great success in building up its own business structure
parallel to the structure of capitalism in distribution and
even in a few branches of productive enterprise.

In the fourth phase, in which we are living to-day, with
the application of science to the methods of production much
more highly organized and spreading fast to the more traditional industries and to agriculture, there is, as we have seen,
a marked tendency for the proportion of the total labour
force engaged in direct production to fall with the increase
in mechanisation, and for the proportion engaged in 'tertiary' occupations to rise. Industry itself employs nowadays

39

relatively fewer direct producers and more office workers and technicians; and at the higher levels there has been an increase both of technologists and research workers and in the number of administrators and managers, each with his subordinate clerks, typists or laboratory assistants. There has been also, with the growth of both machine-minding and office work, a sharp increase in the industrial employment of women—with some tendency for more women to continue in such work after marriage; but this increase in women's industrial (and commercial) employment has been largely offset by the sharp fall in the numbers employed in domestic service. This last has come about not only because high taxation has reduced the proportion of families able to employ domestic help, but even more because the cost of such help has risen sharply in face of better-paid openings in industry and commerce.

Finally, in those countries in which something approaching 'full employment', or even actual shortage of workers in relation to the demand, has now prevailed for a number of years, great strides have been made towards the elimination of what Marx used to call the *lumpenproletariat*—a process of course also greatly aided by the rapid development of the social services under pressure from a popular electorate. With full employment has gone a narrowing of wage differentials and standards of living between the general run of more and less skilled workers, coupled in some of the countries concerned (and notably in the Soviet Union and in the United States) with opportunities for a relatively small minority of highly skilled workers to earn considerably higher incomes than the rest. There has been, in effect, a levelling up from the bottom, a closer grouping of the main body of workers, non-manual as well as manual, in the middle, a spacing out of the upper groups of wage-earners, and an increase in the number of technical and managerial jobs. But there has not been, as we saw earlier, anything that can be appropriately called a 'managerial revolution', though there is an increasing domination of the work processes and of the social stratification derived from them by technological conditions of which the application is increasingly in the hands of research workers and professional engineers.

Near the beginning of the nineteenth century, the Comte de Saint Simon predicted the advent of the age of scientific economic planning and the supersession of *les oisifs* and *les militaires* by *les industriels* as the effective controllers of society; and it was no accident that, though Saint Simon is widely regarded as a pioneer of Socialism, his disciples took an important part in the development of railway building and industrial banking in the France of Louis Philippe and of Napoleon III. *Les industriels*, as Saint Simon regarded them, included the entire class of *producteurs*, as contrasted with all those who claimed to live on the produce of other men's work; and he regarded it as natural that *les grands industriels* should assume the leadership of this class, and was confident that they would use their leadership in the interest of what he called '*la classe la plus nombreuse et la plus pauvre*'. The class struggle, as he envisaged it, was between *les producteurs* and *les oisifs*, not between capitalists and workers—or rather not between managers and workers—for he thought of his *grands industriels* essentially as managers rather than as capital-owners. In the event, the separation of management from ownership did increasingly come about through the development of joint stock enterprise. But the process took a long time, and shows no sign of becoming complete, even to-day, except where public ownership has been generalized as an outcome of revolution. Instead of the anticipated struggle between *les industriels* and *les oisifs*, the nineteenth century produced, under the influence of the Industrial Revolution, the struggle between Capital and Labour, everywhere tangled up with the continuing struggle of the rising middle classes against aristocratic privilege. This economic class struggle, however, instead of becoming more and more simplified by the polarization of classes, as Marx expected in the *Communist Manifesto*, became in the West more and more complicated as a consequence of the increasing differentiation within, and blurring of the lines between, classes under the impact of successive waves of technological advance. Only in Eastern Europe did the Marxist diagnosis of 1848 fit the situation better and better right up to 1917—not because Russian capitalism developed in purer form than the capitalism of the West, but for the very opposite reason that the Czarist political system perverted and distorted its growth by obstructing the development of new classes and the blurring of class divisions which Western Capitalism in varying degrees allowed. To-day, the removal of these obstacles is allowing Soviet social structures to work out a system of differentiation based on productive service which has much in common with that of the United States and of the more advanced areas of Western Europe—but with the immense difference that there is in the Soviet Union no owning class, but only a large range of income differentials based on work done. This politico-economic difference is, of course, of the utmost significance: nevertheless, what has occurred in the Soviet Union since 1917 illustrates, fully as much as what has occurred in America or in Western Europe, the influence of technological forces upon the social structure.

III

The Social Structure of England

I. THE WORKING CLASSES

A FEW years ago, when the British Institute of Public Opinion asked a random sample of grown-up persons of both sexes to what social class they considered themselves to belong, rather less than half of those who answered said that they belonged to the working class. What was at first thought more startling was that those who gave this answer were slightly outnumbered by those who regarded themselves as belonging to the middle classes, only one out of every fifty who were asked designating himself or herself as a member of the upper class. Such answers are of course highly subjective: they tell us, not what class a person does belong to, but how he reacts at a particular time to a question framed in a particular way. In this instance, the result may have been affected by the fact that the persons questioned were given three grades of middle-classness—upper, middle, and lower—to choose from, whereas the entire working class was lumped together without any sub-division. This may have led to some of those who were doubtful assigning themselves to the lower middle rather than to the working-class group; but among those who put themselves in the middle classes more than twice as many chose plain 'middle' rather than 'lower middle' as a designation, and the 'middle' and 'lower middle' together outnumbered the 'upper middle' by nearly seven to one.

It is not at all easy to relate these subjective estimates to any more objective calculation. There was no Population Census in this country between 1931 and 1951; and anyone who has worked on the Census figures knows that it is very difficult to use them as a basis for estimating class distribution. The Census gives no social classification of the unoccupied or the retired; and until 1951 it divided the occupied into the three categories of 'managerial', 'operative', and 'working on own account'—which is not very helpful, as the line between the first and second groups is bound to be difficult to draw and the third group may include anyone from a popular novelist or a successful barrister to a charwoman. The figures of the 1931 census themselves show that the Census classification had then very little relation to the subjective estimations of class-affiliation. Out of twenty-one million 'occupied', it put sixteen millions in the 'operative' group, as against only 1,180,000 in the 'managerial' and 1,272,000 in the 'own account' groups. Among those ranked as operatives were 1,414,000 clerks, typists, and draughtsmen, 733,000 attached to 'professional' occupations, 312,000 in public administration and defence, and 1,329,000 in commercial occupations, including shop assistants. The largest groups in the 'managerial' category were 200,000 in agriculture, presumably for the most part farmers employing labour, 388,000 in commerce and finance (largely shopkeepers), 120,000 in personal service (mainly in garages, hotels, inns, and boarding houses), 64,000 in professional occupations, 57,000 in transport and communications, 53,000 in the metal industries, and 50,000 builders and contractors. Most industries made only a small contribution to the 'managerial' total. The 'working on own account' group again had a preponderance of farmers and shopkeepers, with the professions and personal service categories also well to the fore.

In the Census of 1951 an attempt has been made to present a more realistic picture. The full returns have not yet been published, but the Registrars-General have issued two very useful volumes of statistics based on a one per cent sample of all the returns; and these give for our purposes a sufficiently accurate analysis of the numbers in the various occupations listed, with some attempt to distinguish between employers, managerial employees, supervisors, skilled and less-skilled wage- and salary-earners, and persons working 'on own account'. Moreover, each listed occupation has been assigned

44

to one or another of five 'social classes', ranged in a descending order; and there is also a break-up of the occupational totals into what are called 'socio-economic groups'. These attempts are not wholly successful in showing how many persons, either generally or in each industry or occupation, should be assigned to each 'social class' or 'socio-economic group'; for the compilers have had to treat each listed occupation as an indivisible unit, though in fact many of them clearly cover persons belonging to more than one class or group. Nevertheless, the new data are a great advance on anything that could be derived from earlier Censuses, and do enable those who use them to get a considerably clearer picture of the essentials of class structure.[1]

According to the estimates made on the basis of the Census of 1951, out of a British total of 17,205,500 occupied and retired males, the numbers assigned to the five social classes are as follows:

Class I	567,800	3·3%	Class III	9,035,200	52·5%
Class II	2,542,200	14·8	Class IV	2,826,000	16·4
	Class V	2,234,300	13%		

No parallel classification is given for occupied *females*, because of the difficulty of assigning a social class to unmarried women workers, many of whom work in gainful occupations only for a few years before getting married. It will be seen that by far the largest of the Census classes is Class III, which includes not only manual workers who are regarded as skilled but also the main groups of rank-and-file non-manual workers and most of the supervisory grades, such as foremen. This grouping is evidently too wide to be of much use; but it is hardly practicable from the Census data to break it up into a higher and a lower category. In the study which appears later in this volume I have divided it into two sub-groups—manual workers on the one hand and non-manual and supervisory workers on the other; but these two are to be taken, not as lower and higher, but as roughly parallel. My personal opinion is that the Census figures put

[1] For a much fuller analysis of this material see the study beginning on page 147 of the present volume.

too many manual occupations into the skilled category, and thus tend to swell the size of Class III as against Class IV. But I am not at all sure whether this makes a considerable difference, or only a small one. At the other end of the same Census class, I should have been disposed to transfer supervisory workers to Class II; but this would perhaps have made Class II unduly wide.

The second, alternative grouping given by the Census authorities is in terms not of 'social classes', but of 'socio-economic groups'. This is designed not to rank each occupation in order above or below the next, but to group occupations into a number of categories—actually thirteen —distinguished rather by the nature of their work than by class-attachment. In this grouping farmers and agricultural workers, as two distinct groups, are separated from those occupied in non-agricultural occupations; and the armed forces are also separately shown. The rest of the occupied population is divided into ten groups, as follows: higher administrative, professional and managerial (including large employers); intermediate administrative, professional and managerial (including teachers and salaried staff); shop-keepers and other small employers; clerical workers; shop assistants; personal services; foremen; skilled manual workers; semi-skilled manual workers; unskilled manual workers.

There is also a third alternative grouping, in terms of what is called 'industrial status'. This puts together in a single category all employers, irrespective of the numbers they employ. In the field of management it distinguishes three grades—general managers and directors, managers of branches or primary departments, and managers of office or subsidiary departments. It also distinguishes workers on own account and also the out of work and the retired. The remainder of the occupied population are classified as 'operatives'; but are divided into two groups, one consisting of those assigned to 'Social Classes' I and II, taken together, and the other of the rest. The classification covers both sexes—in all 17,205,500 males and 7,218,700 females, occupied or retired. Out of these 12,106,000 males and 5,633,400 females are characterized as 'Operatives not in Social Class I or II', and a further 1,299,700 males and 761,500 females as 'Operatives in Social Classes I and II'. Employers number 405,900 men and 54,000 women, and the top grade of management 167,000 men and 18,400 women. The two inferior managerial grades together comprise 470,100 males and 92,700 females. 'Workers on own account' number 887,400 males .and 237,200 females. Finally, the retired of all grades are made up of 1,543,300 males and 302,500 females, and the 'out of work' of 326,100 males and 119,100 females. If the 'retired' are excluded, this estimate puts roughly 77 per cent of all the occupied males and nearly 82 per cent of the occupied females into the main 'operatives' grade, which of course here includes non-manual as well as manual workers. Roughly, in terms of status, four out of every five occupied persons are employed operatives not holding managerial positions, and in terms of Social Class a rather higher proportion of all occupied *males* are assigned to Classes III, IV, and V, taken together, and only about 18 per cent to Classes I and II.

These estimates, and also·the more detailed figures given in the subsequent study, fall a long way short of giving a clear picture of the class structure of contemporary British society, not only because they are based entirely on occupational categories, but also because the occupations are in many instances not adequately itemized. The picture can be made a little clearer by invoking the aid of the annual blue book on National Income and Expenditure. This shows, for the year 1953, the distribution by size of the estimated total of 25,300,000 personal incomes in the United Kingdom, counting each married couple as having a common income. According to this estimate, there were in 1953 about 8,410,000 incomes of less than £250 per annum, another 9,240,000 of from £250 to £499, 5,215,000 of from £500 to £749, and 1,360,000 of from £750 to £999, as against a total of 1,075,000 of £1,000 or over. These higher incomes were made up of 790,000 of from £1,000 to £1,999, of 234,000 between £2,000 and £5,000, of 40,000 between £5,000 and £10,000, and of a mere 11,000 in excess of £10,000. All these figures are of gross incomes before deduction of tax. The figures are not complete, for there are a considerable number of income-recipients the size of whose incomes cannot be ascertained; but they give a rough idea of the relative numbers in the upper, middle, and lower income groups. It has, however, to be borne in mind that a substantial proportion of the incomes in the lowest group must be those of minors or young unmarried persons. Most adult male wage-earners are clearly in the second group, from £250 to £499, whereas a high proportion of occupied females will be found in the bottom group. But an appreciable number of male wage-earners now exceed the £500 level, whereas a high proportion of the rank-and-file male blackcoats fall below it. The figures cannot be used to arrive at any clear estimation of economic or social status: they are only another very rough indication of the contemporary structure of classes.

The plain truth is that the social structure of Great Britain and of other developed industrial countries is much too complicated for easy breaking up into stratified social classes. Indeed, whereas Marx prophesied a century ago that with the advance of capitalism social and economic class relations would become more and more simplified into a sharp opposition of *bourgeois* and *proletarians*, with the *petite bourgeoisie* ground to powder between them, the actual march of events both in Western Europe and in the United States has followed a very different course. Marx was not far away from the truth in predicting the continued decline of the class of small master-craftsmen using mainly hand tools whom he regarded as the core of the *petite bourgeoisie*; but he altogether failed to appreciate either the extent to which technical developments would bring into being new types of small-scale business—sub-contractors, electricians, garage-proprietors, etc.—or the effect of large-scale enterprise in multiplying the numbers of salaried managers, technicians, salesmen, and supervisors. Nor did he see the importance of the rise in the numbers of professional and administrative workers outside industry—a process fostered throughout the nineteenth century by the growth of the trading and industrial employers, who made a rapidly increasing call for the services of doctors, dentists, lawyers, schoolmasters and mistresses, governesses, hotel-keepers, secretaries, and so on, as well as for more and better shopkeepers and, much against their will, for an ever-expanding army of public administrators, local as well as national. It is now a well-recognized fact that, as national wealth increases, the proportion of the occupied population that is engaged in actually making things tends to fall, whereas the proportions in distribution, clerical services, and the professions tend to rise. These changes make the class structure, not simpler, but a great deal more complex; and at the same time the necessity of drawing the majority of the recruits for the groups which are rapidly increasing from the family ranks of those which are decreasing or advancing less fast helps to break up the class unity of the family as a social group and creates many families whose individual members are spread out over a number of class groups.

In this brief study I propose to go back a hundred years, to the time when Marx was making his prophecies about the tendencies inherent in capitalist society, and to try to see what the class structure of British society was, broadly considered, at the time of the Great Exhibition of 1851. Of course, the first thing that stands out in the earlier figures is the higher proportion employed in agriculture, which accounted for 2,375,000 occupied persons as against at most a million to-day, though the total population has risen from less than 21 millions to over 49 millions in 1954.[1] With the decline in agricultural employment has gone a great migration from village to town—not to mention the swallowing up of many villages and of much agricultural land by the spread of towns into the surrounding areas. This shift from rural to urban ways of living has in itself meant a vast change in the social composition of the people; for the patterns both of family life and of social relations outside the family are still substantially different in town and country, and movement, chiefly of younger people, away from the villages to the towns or overseas has greatly altered the character of

[1] Ireland, including Northern Ireland, is left out of the figures at both dates.

village life. Moreover, the big town or city is, socially, very different from the small town with the country near at hand; and in 1851, though there had been rapid growth of London and of the industrial areas during the first half of the nineteenth century, most towns were still quite small by the standards of to-day.

A century ago, the only towns with more than 100,000 inhabitants (including those in their suburbs) were London (already over two millions), Liverpool, Manchester, Birmingham, Glasgow, Edinburgh, Leeds, Sheffield, Bristol, Wolverhampton, and Bradford; and of these only the first five had more than 200,000. Only a further twenty or so had more than 50,000. The growth of big towns in the later nineteenth century was increasingly associated with a process of social segregation of rich and poor and even of the main body of the working classes and of the moderately well-to-do. The great age of one-class urban and suburban areas was beginning, with important effects on social relations and on the development of local government; for often the new suburbs were cut off administratively from the towns to which they belonged, so that the municipal areas came to be largely a mixture of working-class houses, factories, and business premises, with many of the better-off inhabitants living outside the areas over which municipal rates were levied. Extension of town boundaries did something, in the long run, to set this right; but in most cases it lagged a long way behind the real growth of the towns. Birmingham was the outstanding exception; but even Birmingham could not be a complete town, because on the west it bumped right into other municipalities—Smethwick and West Bromwich—which maintained their administrative separateness though they had really become parts, with Birmingham, of a single vast city.

The other thing that stands out in any comparison between the social composition of the British people a century ago and now is the immense increase in the numbers of black-coated and professional workers. On this point, I must ask the reader to excuse the absence of any exact statistical comparison: there have been so many changes in the methods of compiling the occupational parts of the Census that no accurate comparisons can be made. Successive Censuses have shown a bewildering tendency to move whole blocks of people from one classification to another, especially such groups as clerks, shopkeepers and shop assistants, and the lower grades of professional workers. Through all the changes, however, the trends remain unmistakable. Clerks and commercial travellers, who were grouped together, in 1851, numbered only 60,000: in the Census of 1951 clerks, draughtsmen and typists added up to nearly two and a half millions. In 1851 the group included no women at all: in 1951 the females numbered 1,428,000, as against 1,030,000 males. Persons engaged in merchanting, shopkeeping and financial occupations numbered about 130,000 in 1851: the most nearly comparable group in 1931 accounted for 2,230,000. Education occupied about 100,000 teachers in 1851 and 356,000 in 1951. The services of Government and Local Government (excluding clerks and professional workers) employed 75,000 in 1851: for 1951 the nearest comparable total is 333,000. The professions, excluding education, added up in 1851 to about 150,000: in 1951 they were well over a million. All these figures are very inexact, because of changes in classification; but I feel sure that the broad impression conveyed by them is correct.

Side by side with this increase in the proportions of black-coated and professional workers has gone a change in the structure of the manual working class. A century ago, the social gulf between skilled craftsmen and labourers was considerably wider than it is to-day. It was greater in incomes, and greater in ways of living and in standards of education and culture. For regular labourers in building and engineering, by no means wholly unskilled types, the weekly wage in the big towns about 1850 ranged from 12s. or less to at most 14s. or 15s.[1] Skilled men on time work got at least half as much again, and this meant a very big difference when the lower rates left no margin over and above sheer necessaries—though of course many who had

[1] Multiply by 3 to 4 to translate very roughly into present purchasing power.

no margin made one at the expense of such necessaries. Educationally, the gulf between craftsmen and labourers was wide: many labourers had hardly been to school at all, whereas most skilled workers had received some sort of formal education and many had supplemented this by attendance at some sort of adult class or Sunday or evening school. Many of the skilled workers were regular chapel-goers, and others belonged to Owenite or Secularist societies or to Mechanics' Institutes or similar agencies for both technical and general education. It is broadly true that, until well after 1850, there was less in common between skilled and unskilled manual workers—I mean in manners and ways of life—than between the former and the small masters and tradesmen for whom many of them worked. It was still fairly common for the skilled craftsman to become a small master; and consequently there were many cases of brothers one of whom worked for wages while the other worked on his own or even employed a few skilled and unskilled men.

A century ago, Trade Unions, save in very exceptional cases, were confined to skilled workers. For a brief period in the 1830s there had been a mass growth of Trade Unions extending to the less skilled; but this movement had been crushed out after the collapse of the Grand National Consolidated Trades Union in 1834, and only the craftsmen's societies, usually on a local basis, had remained in effective existence. The first of the great modern Trade Unions, the Amalgamated Society of Engineers, was actually founded in 1851, but made no attempt to organize the less skilled workers in engineering. In the cotton industry the local societies of spinners and weavers were beginning to link up into larger combinations; but there, too, little attempt was made to bring in the less skilled. The miners had built up for a time in the 1840s a big national Trade Union; but by 1850 it had been crushed out after a series of struggles, and even at its height it had been mainly composed of skilled hewers, with not many of the less skilled workers in its ranks.

Trade Unionism, then, was a force only among a limited labour aristocracy, which was concerned to defend its position against the less skilled workers as well as against the employers, and insisted for this purpose on rules governing the entry to apprenticeship, the number of apprentices, and the exclusive right to practise a skilled trade, to the full extent of its power to enforce its claims. Employers in most of the larger industries were still refusing to 'recognize' Trade Unions as entitled to bargain collectively on their members' behalf, and were denouncing them as obstacles to efficiency because of the restrictive practices which they enforced. In many of the less mechanized occupations, however, the craftsmen's power was great, because they had an effective monopoly of skill; and in such crafts, even without formal recognition, a good deal of collective bargaining occurred. Trade Unionism, in 1850, was still exceedingly unpopular with the middle classes and was continually under attack in the newspapers. Though combination had been made lawful in 1824–5, its exercise was still hemmed in by many legal restrictions, which drove many Unions to secret practices and conspiratorial ways. When the Victorian novelists deigned to mention such matters, they usually took it for granted that their readers would have a strong anti-Trade Union bias. The curious can find a good example in Mrs. Henry Wood's *A Life's Secret* (1867), which contains a vigorous attack on Trade Unionism in the building trades. This mood persisted almost unchanged until the 1870s, when it began to be modified under the influence of the extended legal recognition given to the Trade Unions in 1871—itself a sequel to the enfranchisement of most of the skilled workers in the towns by the Reform Act of 1867. For from that date both the great political parties were under the necessity of wooing the enfranchised section of the working class; and after 1884, when voting rights were much further extended in both town and country, the opinions of the less skilled workers began also to count, though it was not until towards the end of the 1880s that Trade Unions began to spread to any great extent beyond the more highly skilled groups.

It was mainly after this stage had been reached, and as the effects of the generalization of elementary schooling under the Acts of 1870 and 1876 began to make themselves felt, that the gulf between the skilled and a large section of the less skilled workers began to get narrower, in social habits as well as in standards of income. Much has been written about the effects of the Industrial Revolution in destroying craft skill and replacing it by unskilled machine operation; but such generalizations are very misleading. If, by 1850, the power loom had destroyed the traditional craft of handloom weaving, to the accompaniment of deep sufferings among those who were displaced, over the same period power-mule spinning and power-loom weaving had developed as new skilled crafts; and the rise of mechanical engineering, both before and after 1850, brought into existence a wide range of new skills—fitters, turners, pattern-makers, coppersmiths, and a host of others who founded new Trade Unions side by side with the societies of the older crafts. By 1850 this process was in full swing, and, on balance, skills were coming into existence much faster than they were being destroyed. The age of mechanized mass-production was still a long way in the future.

In order to appreciate this point, it should be enough to turn over the fascinating pages of the full catalogue of the Great Exhibition of 1851, or the reports of the juries which awarded the prizes to industrial exhibitors. Whoever does this will soon realize the preponderance of quite small firms and of products made, not in the mass, but individually or by small groups, by processes demanding a high degree of craft skill. As against the craftsmen, the less skilled workers were still for the most part mere labourers, hauling and lifting and doing the heavy, dirty work: the age of the merely dexterous machine-minder, save in a limited range of trades making small consumers' goods, had hardly invaded the main industries using metals as their materials. Birmingham already had its light metal industries producing standard goods at low prices; but a great deal of the work was still done in small workshops with a high proportion of skilled labour.

Women's labour was, of course, already employed extensively in the textile and clothing trades; but in the cotton industry there was only a small preponderance of women

over men, and in the woollen and worsted trades a century
ago the men still outnumbered the women. In the clothing
industries, on the other hand, there were many more women
than men; and the women were also the more numerous in
silk and the lesser textiles. As against this, very few women
were employed in any of the metal trades, except in and
around Birmingham; and in the food preparation trades
there were four men to every woman employed. Nor had
women yet invaded the offices: the influx of women clerks
and typists had not yet begun. There were a good many
women in the distributive trades, but mainly as small shopkeepers: the shop assistants were nearly all men. Apart from
the textile and clothing trades, domestic service was still the
main occupation open to women.

In the middle 'sixties, fifteen years after the date to which
I have been mainly referring so far, the statistician Dudley
Baxter published his well-known study of the distribution of
the national income. Following in the footsteps of Gregory
King towards the end of the seventeenth century, George
Chalmers a hundred years later, and Patrick Colquhoun near
the conclusion of the Napoleonic Wars, Baxter attempted
to divide up the entire population into classes, basing his
division partly on income levels but mainly on differences
of occupation. His figures covered Ireland as well as Great
Britain; but for Great Britain alone he estimated that the
upper and middle classes together numbered 5,562,000 out
of a total population of 24,152,000 (in 1867). This left
18,590,000 for what he called the 'manual labour class'.
Baxter's upper and middle classes thus accounted for 23 per
cent—not far short of a quarter—of the whole people. His
conception of the middle classes was, however, very wide:
he included all clerks and shop assistants, as well as all shopkeepers, in however small a way, two-thirds of the total
number of occupiers of land, a high proportion of the total
numbers occupied in the food and drink trades, and all foremen and supervisory workers, together with the family
dependants of all these groups. Later I shall have something
to say about his break-up of the upper and middle classes
into their main component sections: for the present I am

55

concerned with his sub-division of the working classes. This
he worked out in detail only for England and Wales, and
not for Great Britain as a whole, using as his main criterion
the normal range of incomes in the principal occupations.
This method gave him eight sub-divisions, with average
weekly incomes ranging from 35s. to 12s. Here are his groups,
with the estimated numbers in each.

THE MANUAL WORKING CLASS. ENGLAND AND WALES, 1867

	Average Weekly Wage for Men	Numbers (thousands)			
		Men	Women	Juveniles	Total
1 Most Highly Skilled	35s.	42	2	12	56 ⎫ 1,123
2 Highly Skilled	28s. to 30s.	799	38	230	1,067 ⎭
3 Lower Skilled A	25s.	582	93	201	876 ⎫ 4,695
4 Lower Skilled B	21s. to 23s.	1,030	988	925	3,819 ⎭
5 Unskilled A	15s. to 20s.	260	45	114	419 ⎫
6 Agricultural and Rural Labour	14s.	1,149	127	401	1,676
7 Unskilled B	12s.	108	47	47	202 ⎬ 2,842
8 Unskilled C (all female)	12s. (women)—		447	97	545 ⎭

These figures, of course, refer to income-earners only, and
do not include wives or other dependants not in 'gainful
employment'—to use the familiar phrase of the Census.
They are curious in several respects. In the first place,
Baxter has included in his fourth group, among the lower
grades of skilled workers, all the domestic servants, women
as well as men. These account for nearly 100,000 of the men
included in the group, for no fewer than 692,000 of the
women, and for 387,000 girls and an unknown number of
boys. If we put the boys at 50,000, at the least, and divide
Baxter's fourth group into two sub-groups, we get a very
different-looking result. Thus:

	Average Weekly Wage for Men	Numbers (thousands)			
		Men	Women	Juveniles	Total
4(a) Less Skilled B	21s. to 23s.	931	296	488	1,715
4(b) Domestic Servants	—	99	692	437	1,228

If we now transfer the domestic servants to the third main grouping, where they seem more properly to belong, we get instead of the figures in the final column of the main Table a triple classification as follows :

	Average Weekly Wage for Men	Numbers (thousands)				
		Men	Women	Juveniles	Total	Per cent
A. Highly Skilled	28s. to 35s.	841	40	242	1,123	14·4
B. Lower Skilled	21s. to 25s.	1,513	389	689	2,591	33·3
C. Unskilled and Agricultural	12s. to 20s.	1,616	1,358	1,096	4,070	52·3
		3,970	1,787	2,027	7,784	100

This looks a good deal nearer to reality. How does it compare with the position to-day? There is no comparable estimate, nor do I know of any means of making one from the available data. The nearest thing I know of is an estimate of the status of the entire occupied adult *male* population of England and Wales, classified not by incomes but by 'intellectual requirements', which was made by Sir Alexander Carr-Saunders and Professor Caradog Jones on the basis of the Census of 1931, following the methods used in an earlier calculation by Professor Cyril Burt. This estimate divides the adult males into eight classes, including a bottom group of 'institutional cases' quite below the level of ordinary employability. It runs as follows, in percentages of the adult male population:

1. Highest Professional Work   0·1
2. Lower Professional and Technical   3·0
3. Clerical and Highly Skilled Manual   12·0
4. Skilled Manual and Minor Commercial   26·0
5. Semi-skilled Manual and Poorest Commercial   33·0
6. Unskilled and Coarse Manual   19·0
7. Casual Labour   7·0
8. Institutional Cases   0·2

If we assume that one out of every three persons in the third of these groups is a manual worker, and therefore falls inside Dudley Baxter's conception of the working class, we

E   57

get a triple division of the workers into skilled 34 per cent, semi-skilled 37 per cent, and unskilled 29 per cent—which shows a big increase in the relative size of the skilled group and a big decrease in the unskilled. But this latter classification includes the shop assistants among the skilled workers, whereas Baxter put them into the lower middle class. There is no means of excluding them with any exactitude; but one can say very roughly that, if they were left out, the proportions would be somewhere about 30 per cent skilled, 40 per cent semi-skilled, and 30 per cent unskilled. These proportions, it must be borne in mind, are for adult males only. Baxter's proportions for adult males were 21 per cent highly skilled, 38 per cent lower skilled, and 41 per cent unskilled. It is fairly safe to conclude that the proportion of unskilled workers has fallen, while that of highly skilled manual workers has risen, leaving the middle group of much the same relative size.

There have been, of course, large further changes since 1931, not so much in the degrees of skill required as in the regularity of employment and in the wage-differentials between different grades of workers. At the time of Baxter's survey, 1867, fairly typical wage-rates for skilled engineers and engineering labourers in large provincial centres were 30s. and 15s. or 16s.: the skilled man's rate was nearly twice that of the labourer. By 1914 the comparable rates were 37s. and 24s. or 25s.: the skilled rate was about 50 per cent above the unskilled. By 1952 the skilled engineer's rate in the majority of districts was 129s. and the labourer's 111s.: the difference had narrowed to 16 per cent. No doubt, it was often much bigger for skilled workers on systems of payment by results or in receipt of special bonuses; but many less skilled workers also were on piecework. The differential payment for skill as such had been very greatly reduced. These changes in relative wage-rates were of course part of a wider equalizing tendency—above all, in recent years, of the rise in basic minimum standards due partly to full employment; but they were also partly due to the acceptance of the idea of a minimum standard of civilized life and to the accompanying growth of social security services underpinning this minimum. Socially, the effect has been to bring the less skilled, except a residuum of physical or mental defectives, much closer to the higher sections of the manual working class; and at the same time there has been a much closer approximation in social outlook, as well as in incomes, between the higher wage groups and the lower groups of salary-earners. This is reflected in the spread of Trade Unionism into the blackcoated occupations. Out of about eight million workers affiliated to the Trades Union Congress in 1952, well over a million and a quarter were clerks, shop assistants, postal, or other professional or supervisory workers; and outside the Congress are the big Unions of the teachers, the local government officers, and the higher Civil Servants, as well as a number of bodies representing the lower managerial grades in industry.

These groups on the borderline between the working and the middle classes I must leave over for consideration in the second part of this study. The general conclusion of my argument so far is that over the past hundred years the class composition of society, far from becoming simplified into a stark opposition between capitalists and workers, has become much more complex among the manual workers as well as elsewhere. It is true that the skilled and unskilled manual workers are much nearer than they were to forming a single class; but this has come about as a result of a rise in the lower groups and not at all of a throwing down of the higher groups into the 'increasing misery' that Marx predicted. Nor have the groups ranked socially just above the manual workers been thrown down into the proletariat. To the considerable extent to which they have joined forces with it, the cause has lain rather in an upward assimilation of educational and social standards than in any decline in their economic position. The result is a working-class movement greatly extended at both ends, but the groups which make up this movement are certainly not united by a community of 'misery' or reduced to a common level of 'proletarianism'.

II. THE MIDDLE CLASSES

I pointed out in the preceding section of this study that Dudley Baxter, in 1867, assigned less than a quarter of the population to the upper and middle classes together, and more than three-quarters to the working classes, despite the fact that he assigned all shop assistants, as well as all clerks, to the middle group. As against this I pointed out that in a recent public opinion poll more than half the numbers who answered described themselves as belonging to the upper and middle classes. I do not suggest that the two estimates can be at all closely compared, the later being purely subjective and the earlier an attempt at objective classification; but there is clearly good reason to say that, over the period since Baxter wrote, there has been a big increase not only in the relative numbers working in 'blackcoat' occupations but also in the proportion in the higher and middle ranges of non-manual employment. At any rate, this is true of each sex, taken separately. Among women, the two outstanding developments have been their incursion into the higher ranges of professional work and the vast increase in clerical employment. In most occupations where they work side by side with men women have still to achieve 'equal pay'; but their relative position is a great deal better than it used to be, both in mixed and in purely women's employments, and a high proportion of those who now work in clerical jobs come from the families of manual workers and would have had in Baxter's time no openings in many parts of the country outside domestic service or a few very ill-paid workshop trades. There has been, no doubt, at the same time a very considerable move into non-manual work of young women who, in Baxter's day, would have regarded it as socially degrading to take up any paid employment at all—or whose families would have so regarded it. Nevertheless, the main sources of the new non-manual women's labour have been the children of working-class families or of 'blackcoat' families near in status to the manual working class.

As for men, the entry of women both into industry, outside the textile and clothing trades—in which they have been long established—and into commercial and clerical work has tended on the whole not to oust the men but to push them up higher, by making more supervisory and higher clerical jobs which have been largely filled by men. Moreover, the great increase in the professions has on the whole made much more room for men than for women, despite the very great *percentage* rise in women's employment in these fields. If the two sexes are taken together, the increase is probably numerically greatest in those sections of the working population that lie on the borderline between the working and the middle classes—clerks, typists, shop assistants, and similar groups; but the main process has been one of upgrading all along the line, and the rise in the proportion of higher posts has been very marked.

Having discussed in the first section of this study mainly the changes in the working class over the past century, I have now to say something of the changes in the composition of the upper and middle classes. But of the upper classes it is now exceedingly difficult to speak at all in a significant way. A hundred years ago 'upper class' definitely meant 'gentleman' or 'gentlewoman' and something besides; and the prefix 'gentle' had in most people's minds a definite relation to family antecedents as well as to occupation—or to the absence of it. There was, to begin with, a body of hereditarily titled persons—peers and baronets, with their wives and the peers' children. These, though not a few of the new rich had inter-married with them and a few had been ennobled themselves, still drew the majority of their new recruits—and of their wives when they did not marry among themselves—from a wider group of county families standing next below them in the social hierarchy. These two bodies of persons still constituted primarily a *landed* aristocracy, and the new men whom they accepted into their ranks had usually bought land as a prerequisite to acceptance. But buying land was not of itself enough, even if buying a suitable wife went with it. The appropriate manners had also to be acquired; and the source of wealth mattered fully as much as the amount. A banker, financier or merchant could buy his way in much more easily than an industrial employer: an Indian nabob or West Indian planter was much more readily accepted than a coalowner or ironmaster, unless the latter was also an aristocrat in his own right.

Round this class of landed nobility and landed gentry circled a host of relatives, well-to-do or quite poor, who claimed gentility because of their family connections. They made this claim, even if the lords or squires to whom they were related totally ignored their existence; and it was regarded as a dreadful come-down to inter-marry with anybody outside the charmed circle of gentility. Readers of the Victorian novelists, among whom I count myself as one of the most diligent gleaners of social facts, will know very well how often the plot turns on the horrors of marrying anyone who is not quite a 'gentleman' or a 'lady'. They will remember the fuss about Lady Somebody De Courcy marrying the family attorney and, lower down the scale, continual botherations about ladies and gentlemen who got entangled with persons who were not quite the thing. There is, for example, a story of Mrs. Oliphant's, called *The Railway Man and his Children* and published as recently as 1891, which is largely about the social dilemma of a lady who finds herself led to contemplate marriage, not with an engine-driver or booking-clerk, but with a wealthy and highly intelligent civil engineer who goes about the world designing and superintending the construction of railways. This admirable person is stigmatized socially as a 'railway man', and is regarded as cut off by his calling from the ranks of eligible suitors. True, the lady marries him in the end; but then, Mrs. Oliphant was a highly enlightened woman. She was only describing a widely prevalent sentiment, which she knew her readers would readily accept.

This insistence on gentility, with its pretensions to 'good blood', was buttressed up in Victorian sentiment by a constant harping on the vulgarity of those who were outside the pale of 'society'. From Jane Austen near the beginning of the nineteenth century to Thackeray in the middle of it, the major novelists are full of these imputations of ungentlemanly manners and feelings to all sorts of social climbers; and naturally the ruck of popular writers made even more of the point. The gentlefolk feel themselves to be a class apart, but under perpetual threat of debasement by contact with the upstarts. One of their greatest defences is the Established Church, even though it presents awkward problems of social intercourse with 'not quite ladies' who gate-crash on the good works of the parish and hover round the parson—whom the ladies do their best to regard as an honorary gentleman by virtue of his cloth, even if his secular claims leave something to be desired. The Church is essentially a gentlemanly institution, and its social activity a ladylike pursuit; whereas Dissent is ungentlemanly and even revolting to persons of right feeling. This horror of Dissenters runs through the stories of Charlotte Yonge and of many other Victorian writers, always mixed up with considerations of social class. Miss Yonge was broadminded enough deeply to admire her hero in *The Pillars of the House* who stooped to become a printer, stationer, and local newspaper editor in order to save his brothers and sisters from penury; but he remained a stout Churchman, or he would have forfeited all her applause. Even so, he had to be rewarded by coming into landed property and resuming his rightful place among the gentry; and, though he had prospered in business, the stain could never be wholly wiped out, except in the eyes of God.

A hundred years ago, the 'gentle' class still had no doubts about the rightness of its superior claims, though it had no longer anything like the same near monopoly of wealth and power as it had possessed in the eighteenth century. Side by side with it had grown up the new rich, whose position depended on trade and industry; and this class, with its following of lesser employers, tradesmen, and managerial workers, already dominated the life of the larger towns and the industrial districts and sent its representatives to Parliament in large enough numbers to have considerably altered the tone, and much more the policy, of that once exclusive club. In general, this new higher class, except at the very top, did not yet mingle much in private social relations with the gentry. A large part of it held itself consciously aloof, repelling as well as being repelled. It was predominantly

Nonconformist, hostile to the landed interest, proud of having made its own way in the world and of not tracing its ancestry back beyond a grandparent at most. At the same time, a large part of it was eager to improve its social manners, and especially the manners of its children. Its richer members were beginning to settle down to less abstinent standards of living than they had practised earlier in the century, when capital was hard to borrow and the way to riches lay largely through ploughing profits back into business almost as fast as they were earned. The joint stock era was on the way, with its diffusion of industrial and commercial capital among large bodies of inactive shareholders, and with less need for the active capitalists to scrape and squeeze. From the eighteenth century the business classes had had their Dissenting Academies for the higher education of their own sons, by no means exclusively for the ministry. The nineteenth century saw both a great increase in schools with a commercial bias for middle-class boys and a rapid reconstruction of the old Grammar Schools in the towns to meet middle-class needs. At the top of the scale the new rich were sending more of their sons to the old Public Schools and to the new ones that were being founded in imitation of them, but with a less exclusive social appeal.

It was, in the end, largely through the Public Schools, new and old, and through the reformed and expanded Grammar Schools, that the cultural gulf between the 'gentlefolk' and the new wealthy and well-to-do came to be bridged. There, too, the bridge was built between Churchmen and Dissenters, even though the control of Public Schools and of most Grammar Schools remained chiefly in the hands of Churchmen. Wealthy Dissenters, following the line of least resistance, gradually stopped boycotting schools presided over by headmasters and governors connected with the Established Church, and the schools took to welcoming Dissenters' sons, partly in the hope of converting them into Churchmen as well as into socially presentable persons. There was, after the middle of the century, a gradual drift of more of the new wealthy into the arms of the Church; but there was also a gradual *détente* on both sides, as the

64

manners of the new middle classes came to be more nearly assimilated to those of the gentry.

Yet the social claims and prestige of the gentlefolk died (and are still dying) hard. When the middle classes got votes, and seats in Parliament to go with them, in 1832, there was for a long time surprisingly little change in the social composition of the House of Commons. The new wealthy did not for the most part want to become legislators, or to spend their time away from their business affairs. They only wanted to have a Parliament that would pass the laws they required; and they remained content, for the most part, to let the gentry sit in the House of Commons, provided this condition was met. They had plenty to do locally, in taking the affairs of the reformed Municipal Corporations and the Boards of Guardians into their hands; and though after 1832 they had always a contingent of manufacturers among the M.P.s, it was never very large. Their attitude was on the whole favourable to further extension of the suffrage, because they wanted further voting reinforcement against the aristocracy, which was still well entrenched in many small boroughs as well as in the county constituencies. But even after the Reform Acts of 1867 and 1884, both of which widened the electorate much more than that of 1832, the House of Commons remained largely an assembly of 'gentlemen'. As late as 1900, it contained no fewer than seventy members who were Lords, Baronets, or Honourables, as well as a big contingent of country gentlemen and members of aristocratic families. But by that time the business men outnumbered them. Out of a House of 668, including 83 Irish Nationalists, the employers, bankers, merchants, tradesmen, stockbrokers, and company directors numbered over 250—and there was a good deal of overlapping between this group and the aristocrats.

Side by side with the gentlefolk and the rising business classes there existed, a century ago, a rapidly increasing body of professional men, whose social status was gradually changing. There had been a very wide gulf, for example, in the medical profession between the small body of 'physicians' and 'physicians and surgeons' belonging to the Royal Colleges and the general run of practitioners, commonly called 'apothecaries' and 'surgeons'. The surgeons had their College, but it was open only to a few Fellows: most surgeons were merely licensed. Naval and military service were still common ways of picking up a qualification: only a small proportion of 'doctors' held medical degrees of university standard. The 'doctor' was not, as such, reckoned a gentleman, unless he was one of the privileged few; but his social status was steadily rising with that of the business middle classes, who provided him with more and more of his income. Solicitors, too—still commonly called 'attorneys', with a mildly derogatory social inflection—were rising in social standing as the development of business gave them more and more to do for middle-class clients who were experiencing a similar advance.

The social status of Dissenting ministers remained low, except for a privileged few; but it rose slowly with the increase in national wealth. Earlier in the century it had been not uncommon for ministers of the less prosperous sects to combine their ministry with a manual occupation or with school-teaching; but this practice gradually died out, except for a residue of little chapels that could not sustain a salaried minister even on the most meagre scale. Meanwhile, Church Reform was doing something to narrow the gulf separating the incumbents of rich livings, who had been in many cases pluralists and absentees, from the poor curates who had done most of their work for meagre rewards. Many clergymen of the Established Church, even many incumbents, were still very ill-paid—and are so to-day; but the Reformers inside the Church had set their course by the ideal that every clergyman should be enabled to live as a gentleman, and by the middle of the nineteenth century they had made some real progress, especially in dealing with pluralists and absentees and in insisting on the re-distribution of the revenues of some of the fattest livings.

The new professions that were rising rapidly in social importance raised awkward problems of social status for the old-fashioned. Accountants and bank managers, company managers and managing directors, civil engineers of various types, architects emerging from the ranks of builders, were all developing pretensions to rank with the older professions, and in various degrees were making good their claims. They belonged, however, for the most part rather to the social world of business than to that of the older types of gentlefolk; and the process of assimilation was slow except at the very top. The great railway financiers joined the bankers and merchants at the top of the tree of wealth; and so did the great shipowners, shipbuilders, ironmasters, and colliery proprietors. All these groups drew with them a surrounding body of consultant professionals. But, as against this, the salaries of managers remained for the most part low as long as they were still employees of individual capitalists or small groups of partners. The era of the highly salaried managing director began only with the spread of the joint stock company with its mass of depersonalized shareholders; and the wide acceptance of joint stock enterprise except in a few fields—banking, insurance, and railways especially—came only in the 1870s and 1880s. A century ago, salaried managers were definitely not 'gentlemen': the age of impersonal capitalism was still to come.

Teaching, except at University level and in a very few Public Schools, was a profession—if it could be called one at all—of very low prestige, and was relatively much worse paid than now. Elementary education was developing out of the stage of the monitorial system, under which the older children repeated their lessons to the younger by rote, to the pupil-teacher system, then regarded as a big advance. Dame schools, parish schools, and factory schools in which the teaching was done by unqualified persons—often because they were fit for little else—were still very common: compulsory elementary education in some sort of school recognized as minimally 'efficient' did not come till the 1870s, and it took a long time thereafter to get a tolerable corps of teachers. At the level above the elementary school there grew up, side by side with Public Schools and local Grammar Schools, a host of private venture schools, run for profit, which for the most part paid their assistant teachers wretchedly and took what offered for the money. The State, except for small grants for classes in 'Science and Art', held aloof from secondary education until the Act of 1902, and even thereafter came in but slowly till after 1918. Higher education for girls, which had been stimulated by the foundation of Queen's College and Bedford College in the 1840s, took a long step forward with the establishment of the Girls' Public Day Schools Trust in the seventies; but it lagged a long way behind the growth of new Public Schools for the sons of the middle classes.

Moreover, the classical tradition in higher education was extremely tenacious, and was ardently defended by the Universities and the Church. Despite the efforts of men such as Huxley, who fought hard for recognition of the cultural value of science, the social prestige of science teaching remained low, and it grew up largely outside the Public Schools. This reacted on the social status of the scientists, among whom only a small upper group could lay claim to a 'gentlemanly' education. The University of London, founded in 1826, did something, as an external examining body, to set scientific standards, which were presently taken up in the provinces as local Colleges with a technical bias developed into University Colleges and presently grew to the stature of Universities. But this development falls mainly into the last quarter of the nineteenth century and into the period after 1900.

If we compare the position and structure of the upper and middle classes a century ago with what exists to-day, the first notable difference lies in the shrinkage, relatively, of the upper class. The titled aristocracy remains, but has been immensely diluted by the ennoblement, not only of a host of country gentlemen in the Victorian era, but also since then of a much greater host of successful business men, followed, latterly, by a cohort of Trade Union and Co-operative leaders. The House of Lords is still overwhelmingly Conservative: it is still predominantly an assembly of wealthy men; but it is no longer a one-class institution. The peerage as a whole is no longer, under the Crown, the top layer of an aristocracy: baronets are to-day, socially, a much more exclusive order than peers. Moreover, the landed aristocracy is no longer nearly so much as it used to be the point of focus for a vast circle of second, third, and fourth cousins. There are still places, especially genteel residential hotels, where ladies proudly reveal their kinship to Lord Somebody; but the more active and self-supporting kinsmen of the nobles and county families have increasingly cut themselves adrift from social dependence on family connections and have come to prefer standing on their own feet, or at any rate to think more of their old schools and colleges than of their family affiliations. This is partly an outcome of the educational assimilation of the upper and upper middle classes; but it is also the result of a decreased will and ability on the part of the gentry to subsidize poor relations in order to prevent them from disgracing the family by entering into ungentle-manly occupations.

In effect, as a social class of really national significance, the upper class has nearly ceased to exist, though much is left of its snob appeal. For practical purposes, the great majority of those who used to feel they belonged to it, even as mere hangers-on, have become merged into the middle classes, and would now think of themselves as 'upper middle class'. Of to-day's really rich, the majority would not natur-ally think of describing themselves as 'upper class'—much less as 'aristocrats': they, too, would describe themselves as 'upper middle class.' Socially, the men of big business mix with the survivors of the old aristocracy on terms of equality, but without complete fusion. Intermarriage causes them to overlap, and the descendants of the rich of yesterday are often indistinguishable from the old aristocrats. But the active financiers and industrialists are, socially speaking, a mixed bunch, and many of them have more in common with the lesser industrialists and business managers than with the public school and university men with whom they rub shoulders in both political and economic affairs. They remain, and prefer to remain, middle class in outlook; and often they look askance at the 'intellectuals', who, much more than they, have taken over the accents and manners of the lesser gentlefolk of a century ago.

The 'intellectuals', as ever, are difficult to place in the

social hierarchy. The growth of secondary education on a selective basis, with a strong literary bias taken over from the older Public Schools and Universities, has added very greatly to their numbers; and they have found a great many new professional openings, above all in journalism and authorship, in publishing and in the public services, in higher teaching and broadcasting and script-writing and acting, and in representing Great Britain, publicly or privately, in a host of capacities overseas. Until quite recently, although recruits from below were continually pressing up into the intellectual occupations, in most of them there was a great advantage still on the side of the products of the greater Public Schools and of the older Universities. But to-day the composition of the 'intelligentsia', in respect of social origins, is changing fast as a consequence of the rapid development of state and state-aided secondary schools—now re-named Grammar Schools—and of the newer Universities. The higher intellectual positions are no longer a prerogative of young people coming from higher professional or other well-to-do middle-class homes. The sons of clerks, miners, small tradesmen, and even of less skilled workers can reach them; and, in much smaller numbers and over a narrower field, the daughters as well.

. This makes the intellectuals of the present day a group of widely differing social origins. But, in comparison with the intellectuals of a century ago, they hold a much more stable position in the social system. The immense growth of the Civil Service, of the higher branches of education, and of the social services generally, has created a wide range of salaried positions for the intellectual 'aristocracy', and has made Grub Street and the whole tribe of the disappointed as described in George Gissing's novels obsolete. The struggling artist no doubt remains: the struggling intellectual in these days can usually find himself a not ill-salaried retreat from adventure. At any rate, the intellectuals in the main live much less precariously than they used to do, despite the increase in their numbers.

Moreover, there has been a great growth of higher education in the sciences and in mathematics. The older 'Public'

Schools, as well as the new Grammar and Technical Schools, have developed scientific teaching; and there has been a very great increase in the openings for scientists and technicians in many kinds of professional work, including research and teaching as well as technological employment in industry and in the public services. There is, indeed, to-day a marked shortage of highly qualified scientists, especially in the field of education; and special measures have been taken to expand science teaching in the Universities and to develop the Technical Colleges sponsored by local Education Authorities and to supplement them by providing greater opportunities for higher technological training. The old classical tradition has shown a remarkable tenacity in face of this challenge and is still strongly entrenched in the 'Public' Schools; but the growth of state-provided secondary education has brought with it a great advance not only in the teaching of science but also in that of history and the social studies. Schools, as well as Universities, have been compelled to provide more diversified courses, not only because specialization has increased, but also because many new subjects have been winning their way to educational recognition.

All the groups that I have been speaking of so far make up, however, only a fraction of what is meant by the middle classes, the bulk of whom are neither intellectuals nor professionals of any sort nor products of the Public Schools. Farmers and retail tradesmen, and the middle sections of the Civil and Local Government services and commercial concerns, are still by far the most numerous groups outside industry; and in industry there are the technicians, the middle and lower ranks of management and administration, the small employers, and, on the borderline the foremen, forewomen, and supervisors of the manual productive processes, and the analogous grades in the transport services. Farmers, after a bad period in the second half of the nineteenth century and a slow recovery in the early years of the twentieth, have improved their economic position faster than any other considerable section of the occupied population. Income from farming, according to the Government's figures in the National Income White Paper, had risen from £60 millions in 1938 to £389 millions in 1952; and these gains have been on the whole well spread among large and small farmers and over the main areas of the country. The small holder or small farmer who employs little or no labour outside his own family lives a laborious life; but his economic circumstances and his security have improved greatly, and the large farmers have risen even more markedly in the social scale.

Shopkeepers, too, have done well as a class, with quick turnover, no spoilt or unsaleable stocks, and a great decrease in bad debts. Like farmers, they grumble at the high cost and scarcity of hired labour; but there can be no doubt about their improved standards of income and security. Their position is, no doubt, rather less well assured than that of the farmers; for, whereas it would be more necessary than ever to sustain agricultural output in a depression, a fall in employment would react immediately on the position of the retail traders, especially in the non-food trades. But, as matters stand, both farmers and tradesmen have been able to advance their relative standards of living and in many cases to put away money or emancipate themselves from the burden of debt. The Civil Servants, the Local Government Officers, and the non-industrial salary-earners generally have fared less well in terms of incomes and standards of living since 1939; but in comparison with their position a century ago, the improvement is marked, especially in the middle ranges. In industry the grades nearest the summit have probably done best, with the big increase in highly salaried positions. Contrary to a commonly held opinion, even big business is not generous in its salary payments to the lower managerial grades, and promotion is often a long time in coming, if it comes at all; but here, too, there has been a great increase in security of employment, both among technicians and lesser managers and among supervisory employees. The foremen and supervisors, when they are on time work, have indeed in many cases lost ground in income in relation to skilled pieceworkers whom they superintend; but in a growing number of instances their position has been rectified by various forms of overhead bonus based on work-shop output. Socially, the supervisors are for the most part not sharply marked off from the skilled manual workers; and this holds good also for a high proportion of the routine technicians who play an increasing part in the newer indus-tries that have a basis in modern scientific techniques. A part of the educational revolution of our times that is often overlooked is the growth of technical courses—for National and Higher National Certificates and the like—in Technical Colleges and specialized institutions of Technology. For more than half a century there has been in the making a new, non-literary educated class, or sub-class, of minor professional workers who, still playing only a small part in the older industries, wax continually in numbers and importance in those industries in which the applied sciences supply the very foundation for productive techniques.

These lower ranges of the middle classes fall very broadly into two sections—the salary-earners and the profit-makers. The farmers and retail tradesmen constitute the main body of the second group; and the nature of their incomes has a big effect in determining their political and economic affilia-tions. Though the Labour Party has done a great deal to benefit the farmers, it does not easily win their votes; and though retail traders have done well economically under state control, they still vote mainly for the Conservative Party. The salary-earners, on the other hand, have provided many more converts to Trade Unionism and to political Labour, partly because salaries have become much more a matter for collective bargaining, except in the higher ranges of industry and commerce, but also because there is less educational and cultural difference than there used to be between most salary-earners, outside the higher professions, and the more skilled manual workers. The salary-earners are, however, an unstable political force: it is clear from the figures of the General Elections of 1950 and 1951 that a good many of them, after voting for the Labour Party in 1945, again changed sides. Otherwise Labour would have lost fewer seats in the dormitory suburbs, especially in Greater London.

I wish there were some way of measuring satisfactorily the actual numbers of these two middle groups of small profit-makers and small salary-earners. But there are almost none, even if we use the new data supplied by the Census of 1951. We know from that source that in 1951 there were in England and Wales 624,000 proprietors and managers of retail businesses, as compared with 907,000 shop assistants— not quite one assistant and a half tô every proprietor or manager. We know that there were 317,000 farmers and farm managers and 525,000 farm labourers, and that roughly 37 per cent of the farmers were classified as employers or managers, and 63 per cent as working 'on their own account'. We know that 1,387,000 persons were classified as professional workers, including 357,000 teachers and 240,000 sick nurses; and we can give the numbers in the main higher professions. What we cannot do, in any satisfactory way, is to find out the real numbers and status of the intermediate grades in industry, including both lesser managerial and supervisory workers; for even the improved Census classification into 'Social Classes' is for this purpose of little use in a large number of occupational groups. It gives, for some of the main industries, very widely differing ratios of 'managerial' and higher grades personnel to 'operatives', ranging from 2 per cent of those occupied in coal mining to 13 per cent in chemical manufacture, and more than 15 per cent in the electrical trades. In part, the differences reflect the presence or absence of large numbers of small entrepreneurs; in part they depend on the technological structure. To a sufficient extent to make any conclusions unsafe, the classifications are arbitrary; and they give no clue to the numbers in the supervisory as distinct from the managerial grades—though, for most industries, the number of supervisors can now be separately estimated. For what the figures are worth, they show, over all industries, a division of personnel into 3 per cent employers and higher managers, 2·5 per cent lesser managers, 9·5 per cent high-grade operatives and 5 per cent working on their own account, and 80 per cent 'other operatives'. For the coal mines, which show the lowest percentage of 'managerial'

74

workers, the supervisory grades, at 7·5 per cent of the whole, are four times as numerous as the 'managers' and high-grade operatives combined; but this proportion is not likely to be representative of industry generally.[1]

The only other line of quantitative approach to the question is through the study of the distribution of personal incomes as now given in the annual White Paper from which I have quoted already—recently supplemented by some exceedingly valuable figures published since 1950 in the annual Reports of the Commissioners of Inland Revenue.

The Inland Revenue Report now makes it possible to break up these figures in a more revealing way. From it we get the following particulars of numbers of pre-tax incomes above Income Tax level in 1938–9—£125 in that year—and the total number of incomes in 1953.

	1938–9 (thousands)	1953	Rise %
£125 or £135–£150	2,483 }	8,410 (under £250)	
£150–£250	4,600 }		
£250–£500	1,890	9,240	389
£500–£750	390	5,215	1,238
£750–£1,000	149	1,360	813
£1,000–£1,500	130	600	361
£1,500–£2,000	52·7	190	261
£2,000–£3,000	46·2	145	214
£3,000–£5,000	33·2	89	168
£5,000–£10,000	18·2	40	120
£10,000–£20,000	5·6	9	61
Over £20,000	2·1	2	—5

The changed value of money, of course, makes these figures incomparable as they stand, and accounts for a large part of the increase in the total number of incomes over £250, and also for a large part of the shift from lower to higher income grades. The group getting between £250 and £500 now includes the main body of adult male manual workers; and some of these have mounted into the next higher groups. The percentage increase in the numbers of incomes at the various levels shows a continuous decline from its peak in the

[1] For a further analysis of the managerial and kindred groups, see pages 159 ff.

range £500–£750; but the fall does not become very steep until the highest levels are reached. Even at the range £2,000–£3,000 the number of incomes had more than trebled, and even at £3,000–£5,000 it had more than doubled. If we take the cost of living for the well-to-do classes as having roughly doubled between 1939 and 1953, and ignore changes in total population, we get the following comparisons. There were 539,000 pre-tax incomes of £500–£1,000 in 1938–9; and there were 790,000 incomes of £1,000–£2,000 in 1953. Incomes of £1,000–£2,000 numbered nearly 183,000 in 1938–9; incomes of £2,000–£5,000 numbered 234,000 in 1953. There had been some fall in the gross real incomes of the well-to-do, as distinct from the very rich; but their numbers had not been greatly reduced. What had made the real difference had been the much heavier incidence of taxation at the higher levels, much more than any change in incomes before taxation.

Thus, according to the figures given in the National Income Blue Book, whereas the persons in the income group £250–£499 retained in 1953 after direct taxation 96·5 per cent of their gross incomes, and those in the group £1,000–£1,499, retained 83·2 per cent, those with incomes of £5,000–£9,999 kept only 45·5 per cent and those with incomes exceeding £10,000 only 30·4 per cent. These proportions, to be sure, take no account of indirect taxes, which fall more heavily on the smaller incomes; but even when allowance is made for them, the effects of taxation on the distribution of real incomes has clearly been very substantial.

As for the future, it is possible only to suggest certain clearly defined trends. The educational policies to which Great Britain stands committed under the Butler Education Act of 1944 involve an increasing equalization of opportunity, though not by any means a complete levelling—for they leave the, 'Public', Schools intact, and we are still a very long way off 'parity of esteem' between the different types of state secondary school, even apart from wide disparities in actual ages at leaving. The trend is, however, clearly towards a lessening of educational inequality and towards a wider diffusion of opportunity for the gifted children of poor

76

parents. The trends in industry involve a progressive increase in the number of scientifically trained workers, and therewith a further expansion of technical education. The high level of taxation on the middle and higher incomes, which is irreversible in view of the commitment of all parties to the expansion of the social services, involves a squeezing of the spending power of those sections of the middle classes whose gross incomes are least expansible—especially the salary-earners outside industry and the possessors of smallish un-earned incomes; and this factor makes in favour of increasing educational and social assimilation between these groups and the upper strata of the manual workers and clerical employees. These prospects, however, fall a long way short of threatening any important section of the middle classes with impending ruin or even serious social decline. The rise of the working classes has not been, on the whole, at the expense of the middle classes: it has been much more a social levelling-up than a levelling-down, except for the really wealthy. Six years of Labour Government did not materially alter the social structure, except at the two extreme ends. Beyond this I do not feel disposed to prophesy: the entire world outlook, and Great Britain's part in it, are too uncertain to make even guessing worthwhile.

IV

The Conception of the Middle Classes

IN these days, when the desire for exact statistical measurement has taken so strong a hold on men because of its positive achievements in the realms of natural science, it is not to be wondered at that some sociologists have set out hopefully to measure the magnitude of the middle classes. There are two ways in which such measurement has been attempted. The one is to begin with a definition of the social groups which are deemed to belong to the middle classes, and thereafter to use the available demographic material for forming an estimate of the numbers of persons included in these groups. This method, however good the statistical data may be, is bound to yield results which differ widely according to the definition adopted by the person making the estimate. Nor is this simply a matter of including or excluding certain entire doubtful groups, such as shop assistants or works foremen and supervisors. It is also a matter of drawing the line at this or that point within particular groups, in which some members seem clearly to belong to the middle classes and others not. Farmers and shopkeepers, clerks and typists, and retired or disabled persons living on pensions or small savings are obvious examples. As the groups whose inclusion in the ranks of the middle classes is most doubtful are also, in many societies, the most numerous, the precise points at which the lines are drawn make a vast difference to the result. All that emerges from the use of this method is the conclusion that, in modern civilized countries, the class structure is exceedingly complex, and that any classification involving the notion of a 'middle class' or of an identifiable constellation of 'middle classes' is bound to be arbitrary, and to be quite lacking in scientific precision.

By this method, we cannot really count the middle classes

78

at all: we can only arrive at a very rough estimate of the numbers of persons included in the groups and sections of groups which the particular investigator has decided to assign to the middle classes. The second method, on the other hand, does enable the investigator to give an answer which is not the result of his personal assessment of what constitutes a member of the middle classes. It is the familiar method of question and answer. The investigator draws up a list of classes, which he can make more or less elaborate, on the assumption that social classes can be designated as 'upper', 'middle', and 'lower', or 'working', with more or fewer sub-divisions, such as 'upper-middle' and 'lower-middle', within the three main categories. He and his assistants then present this list to a random sample of persons, asking them to say to which division and sub-division they consider themselves to belong. The resulting answers do at any rate tell us how a random sample of the people—provided the sample *is* random—respond to such a question at a particular time. The results are apt to be somewhat startling at first sight. In the British Institute of Public Opinion's poll, taken in 1948, no fewer than 47 per cent of those asked assigned themselves to one or another sub-division of the middle classes, as against 46 per cent who assigned themselves to the working class, and 2 per cent who regarded themselves as belonging to the 'upper class': 5 per cent did not answer. In Canada in a similar poll in 1948 no fewer than 65 per cent claimed to belong to the middle classes: in the United States a *Fortune* poll of 1940 recorded a 'middle-class' percentage of 79, while in a Gallup poll of 1939 the 'middle-class' proportion rose to 88. In all these American cases, however, those who admitted to being below the 'middle-class' level had to describe themselves as belonging not to the 'working class' but to the 'lower class'; and this almost certainly made a very big difference. But even if, on this account, we ignore the American polls, an assignment of nearly half the population to the middle classes has an air of unreality; for even the widest of the arbitrary definitions used by sociologists would certainly not assign to the middle classes more than about one-third of the British population.

The difference between the two methods just described rests, of course, on a difference concerning the very nature of what is being measured. Are the middle classes to be defined in terms of subjective states of feeling or of objective criteria of income, occupation, family connections, or any other factors that may be considered to be relevant to the determination of class? For some purposes, the class to which people feel themselves to belong may be a matter of considerable sociological importance; but it is not easy to tell how stable such feelings are, or how significant a response the answers can be taken to indicate. The British poll of 1948 gave those questioned three choices within the middle classes —upper middle, middle, and lower middle—as against only a single category of working class, no distinction being made between skilled workers and labourers, or even between workers in regular employment and the groups at the very bottom of the social scale. Such a formulation might well induce a good many who would instinctively have accepted the label of skilled craftsmen or non-manual workers to assign themselves to the 'middle' or 'lower middle' class rather than to the bottom group, however named. As far as I know, no one has attempted a poll in which no labels are given by the investigators, but each individual is simply asked to say to what class he and she feel themselves to belong. Even if this were done, it is most unlikely that any very clear picture of the state of feeling would emerge; for there would almost certainly be a very wide variety of unclear and overlapping designations. These might present a more valid account of the true state of feeling about class, in all its confusions; but they would leave the investigator who is in search of objective measurements entirely unsatisfied.

The conclusion, then, is that very little can be achieved by attempting to measure the size of the middle classes, or of any groups into which they may be broken up for purposes of study, either by using the available statistics of incomes and occupations or by questioning people directly about the class to which they deem themselves to belong. We can find out easily enough by the first method how many people belong to certain unquestionably middle-class professions;

but these islands of certainty cover only a very small part of the total which even the narrowest conception of 'middle-classness' would bring within that designation. The rest is uncertainty, as far as statistical measurement by either of these methods is concerned.

Even though we cannot, by either of these methods, arrive at any valuable estimate of the size of the 'middle class', that does not mean that 'field work' in this kind of study need be unrewarding. It is not without value to find out how many people, and still more what kinds of people, will describe themselves as 'middle class' if they are asked—provided that in using their answers due attention is paid to the precise wording of the question. Moreover, a good deal more can be learnt by asking people how they 'classify' their neighbours and other people they know, or know of. Such questions can help to give clues to the nature of the concept of 'class' in the minds of different persons, and of different kinds of persons; and it is also possible to enquire directly into the stigmata which different people regard as designating class, and into the associations which the idea of class calls up most strongly into their minds. It is possible to ask people directly what they think is meant by 'class', and to analyse the answers so as to discover how far members of the same social groups tend to give the same definitions, or members of different groups different definitions. It is possible to study group behaviour for signs of common class outlooks and actions on the part of members of professions, trades, income groups, and so on, and to treat the data thus obtained by a number of statistical techniques, with useful results as long as the statistician keeps his sense of proportion and does not let his love of such things as correlation coefficients run away with him. A great deal can be done to study the middle classes by modern methods of field work and statistical analysis. What cannot be done is to *count* them in any even approximately objective sense. Fortunately, however, such statistical measurement is not everything—or nearly as much as the more enthusiastic 'social scientists' would have it to be.

Let us, then, put the statistics behind us, and consider the concept itself. The very term 'middle classes' implies the notion of a society divided into classes, and at least suggests a main division into three—upper, middle, and lower. How far does such a division into three main classes correspond to reality either in the present-day societies of Western Europe or America, or in these societies at the successive stages of their development? How far does it correspond to reality in other societies, either of the present or of the past? For any society, at any time, the fit is evidently loose; but it is also evidently very much better for some societies at certain stages of their development than for others or for the same societies at other stages. It fits best, on the whole, either a free City at the height of medieval development, or a highly industrial-ized country at a middle stage of capitalist development, such as Great Britain had reached during the second half of the nineteenth century, or, in a quite different way, a rural structure based on a mingling of landlordism with large and small scale farming. It fits much less well either most forms of relatively primitive society, or the types of society in which feudalism and industrial capitalism are intricately intermingled, or, I should say, the highly diversified social structures which have been characteristic of West Euro-pean and American societies in their most recent phases of change.

It seems most convenient to begin by considering, not what is to be called 'middle class', but the part of society that is regarded as meriting to be called 'upper class'. Where there exists a recognized aristocracy, labelled by its possession of land or of mercantile wealth and of privileges attached to such possession, by way either of titles or of offices or of status in gild or municipal bodies, the main body of the upper class can be easily identified, though there may be much dispute about its exact limits. In the familiar case of aristocracies based on landed property, there are usually a small number of great families, extending outwards through the house-holds of younger sons and the marriages of daughters outside the inner circle, so that the feeling of kinship to the great extends far beyond the reality of greatness. Side by side with these great houses are the families of lesser landowners—*anglicé*, squires; and these in turn throw off shoots of aristocratic sentiment, and sometimes intermarry with the less eligible members of the great families. There may be considerable rivalries and wide differences of culture between the members of these landholding classes; but, whenever they are faced with the rise of claims to social status and privilege resting not on land but on commercial or industrial wealth they tend to be thrown together on the basis of a common claim to be regarded as 'gentlefolk', and to develop a common standard of manners and, up to a point, education, in the hope of marking themselves off from their plebeian rivals. Where, mainly for money's sake, they intermarry with the new rich, they feel a sense of degradation which can be removed only by the assimilation of the new recruits to the family to its standards and outlook on life. Of course, some aristocracies are much more closed than others —some, in theory at any rate, altogether closed. Where access is more open, we have the familiar spectacle of the upstart merchant buying land, setting up as a country gentleman, and perhaps in due course preparing the way for the family to achieve ennoblement.

Merchant aristocracies, which are a product of great trading centres, are usually much less closed than aristocracies based on land. They can, indeed, especially in City-States, close their ranks to a considerable extent and establish great hereditary merchant dynasties almost as exclusive as the landed nobility can achieve. This possibility, however, is greatly restricted by the development of national, as against town, or city, economies; for even though the United States has its Morgans, Rockefellers and Vanderbilts, and France its *deux cent familles*, neither of these can properly be described as constituting an 'upper class' to the exclusion of everyone else. They are groups, rather than classes—at most subsections of a wider top layer of society.

In unified national societies, a merchant aristocracy cannot constitute a closed order. It has, indeed, on the national plane, to do battle with the strongly entrenched landed aristocracy in order to establish its claim to rank at all, as a group, with the upper class. It infiltrates into this class by individual promotion, and does not, save under very exceptional conditions, join it as a group. Up to what we call the 'Industrial Revolution', the numbers of capitalists knocking at the doors of aristocracy were always manageably small: the rise of industrial capitalism based on coal and steam with the accompanying techniques of large-scale production created for the first time a large body of wealthy men, with gradation upon gradation of lesser riches below them, who could vie in pride of possession with the landed and merchant classes, and indeed outvie all but the greatest of the older aristocracy, but were neither assimilable in manners to the existing upper class nor desirous of joining it. These new men emerged distinctively as a middle class, conscious of their difference both from the gentry and from the main mass of the people below their economic level. Whereas the existing aristocracy depended for its upper-classness only in part on wealth or economic position, and quite largely on heredity and family connections, the rising class of industrialists was differentiated at the outset almost exclusively by its economic position as the driving and directing force in the new forms of business enterprise. Individuals here and there might set out to climb out of this class into the aristocracy; but in the main the new men wished, not to become aristocrats, but to achieve political as well as economic influence for their own collective values. They fought against aristocratic privilege, as well as against claims from the mass of the people which seemed to threaten the processes of wealth-accumulation by which they had risen to economic authority. The industrial capitalists thus came to form, on a national scale, a conscious middle class, or at any rate the economic nucleus of such a class. Some of them wished to overthrow the classes above them, and to take their place. Most, at the stage I am here describing, wished only to be assured that the State would order society in conformity with their interests, and were too occupied with their own affairs to wish to take the exercise of political authority directly into their own hands. They were content for the aristocrats who sided with them to do most of the governing and to continue to regard themselves as the upper class, provided that the government did not govern too much, and protected their property against level-

lers from below as well as against extortions in the interest of
the old aristocratic class.

This advancing middle-class group speedily produced its
effects on other parts of the social structure. With its expanding consuming power and rising standards of living it transformed the market for consumers' goods and services. It
needed many more superior shopkeepers and master craftsmen to minister to its needs, and brought into being a host of
shops which set out to do a predominantly middle-class trade.
At the same time, it required more attorneys and solicitors,
more medical men a cut above the ordinary country surgeon
or apothecary, more ministers of religion, especially in Great
Britain of nonconformist persuasions, and presently more
schoolmasters and schoolmistresses capable of giving its children a sound, middle-class education. The professions and
the superior tradesmen, hitherto mainly dependent on upper-
class custom, came to provide more and more for middle-class
needs, and became therewith themselves more and more
'middle class'. The professional elements in the population
became a much larger fraction of the whole, and at the same
time much more mixed in social origin and outlook. Apothecaries, attorneys, and the top layers of the teaching profession
turned into a sort of middle-class gentlemen, and came much
nearer in social status to barristers, clergymen, and army
officers—the old trilogy of gentlemanly professions. But the
new professions—civil engineers, railway technicians, and
dissenting ministers—remained much less gentlemanly in
social estimation, and much more akin to the various grades
of essentially middle-class industrial employers.

Then two further things happened. In England, at any
rate, the public schools, greatly increased in numbers,
brought about a steadily increasing assimilation of outlook
and manners between the children of the lesser members of
the older aristocracy and those of a large section of the new
middle class; and over the same period the spread of the
joint stock system, which greatly fostered large-scale enterprise, brought into existence a new large class of salaried
managers and administrators, not only in mining and manufacture, but also in banking, insurance and commerce. The

educational process speedily made it impossible to tell at sight or by speech who was a 'gentleman' according to the traditional aristocratic reckoning, and who was not. The rise of the salaried element in business, partly replacing small independent master-craftsmen and employers but mainly an additional growth, reinforced the larger capitalists with a considerable group whose prospects, equally with their own, were bound up with the success and expansion of large-scale industrial enterprise. Moreover, the joint stock system immensely multiplied the number of small investors who, playing no active part in the businesses to which their money was made over, lived partly on earnings and partly on the income from their invested savings. Almost the entire professional class became an investing class as well, and thus acquired a stake especially in the larger-scale forms of capitalist enterprise.

These later developments were still at an early stage when Marx formulated, in the 1840s, his theory of the historical evolution of the class struggle. In *The Communist Manifesto*, as well as elsewhere, Marx insisted that, whereas class struggles had existed in all historical ages, the essential characteristic of capitalism was to reduce to two only the classes between which the struggle for power would be finally fought out, with the propertyless proletariat, or working class, as the destined victor. At a time when, in the more advanced countries, the middle elements in society were in fact increasing more than ever before in both numbers and influence, Marx represented these elements as in process of being relentlessly crushed out by the advance of capitalism, which on the one hand flung more and more of the master-craftsmen and small employers down into the proletariat and on the other 'concentrated' capital into fewer and fewer hands with the rise of great combines, and subordinated to itself what was left of the old aristocratic classes, whose hordes of feudal retainers it transformed into a new host of obedient business subordinates, factory slaves, and obsequious ministers to its material and spiritual wants. Marx, thinking despite his labours among British blue-books largely in German terms whenever his mind turned to the main body of the middle

86

classes, regarded the *petite bourgeoisie* as a class in process of extinction because he thought of it as dependent on obsolescent techniques of small-scale production. As for the rapidly growing new groups of managers, supervisors, technicians, and professional workers, far from regarding these as a new and important factor in the class struggle, he dismissed them as mere servants of the *grande bourgeoisie*, able to play no independent rôle in social evolution but only to serve as the commissioned and non-commissioned officers of the army of large-scale capitalism, and to be relied on not to mutiny because it was to their own, as well as to their masters', interest to hold the proletariat—which Marx envisaged as the great majority of the people—firmly at bay.

In Marx's view, then, there were, from the standpoint of the future, only two historically significant classes—capitalists, or *bourgeoisie*, and proletariat. The leading section of the *bourgeoisie*, originally the leaders of the middle classes against the aristocracy, had developed in the advanced capitalist countries into the true upper class, absorbing into itself such elements of the old upper classes as it did not push arrogantly aside, and flinging down into the proletariat its erstwhile allies—the *petite bourgeoisie*—who had failed to make themselves masters of the higher capitalistic techniques. Of course, Marx did not say that this process was anywhere complete: he announced it only as an historical tendency of economic development. He did, however, think that what was left of the 'middle classes'—middle, that is, between the higher *bourgeoisie* and the working class—was made up of heterogeneous elements incapable of following an independent policy. Some of them he regarded as standing for obsolete methods: others as mere camp-followers of the advancing capitalist class. He took no account of the effect of the joint stock system in diffusing throughout the middle groups a share in the ownership, as distinct from the control, of large-scale industry; and, far from giving any countenance to technocratic notions or to the allied notion of the so-called 'managerial revolution', he stressed the increasing dominance of financial over industrial capitalism, and anticipated a growing concentration of capitalist power in the hands of a small class of financial manipulators concerned with the processes of production only as means to money-making on the grand scale.

This Marxian theory in effect involved a splitting of the middle class, at the point of its decisive victory over the old upper class, into contending factions representing the one a progressive and the other a reactionary relation to the powers of production. But the progressiveness of the *grande bourgeoisie* was, in Marx's view, confined within the limits consistent with the continued capitalist exploitation of the rest of the people, and was destined to turn into reaction when its imperative need for continued expansion came up against the obstacle of the limited consuming power which it allowed to its victims. This was to be the 'final contradiction of capitalism', which would lead to its overthrow by the revolutionary proletariat, condemned to 'increasing misery' in the midst of potential plenty. Firm in his conviction that political power could only reflect and not generate economic power, Marx had no idea that popular education and the extension of the franchise could lead, without social revolution, in the direction of positive reforms that would so far limit capitalist exploitation as to bring about a significant re-distribution of income between rich and poor, and to compel all parties aiming at political authority by constitutional means to bid one against another by offering instalments of welfare and gradually transforming the 'police State' with which he was familiar into the 'welfare State' which is to-day at various stages of development not only in Western Europe and the British Dominions, but also in the intensely capitalistic United States. Nor did he anticipate that this growth of political democracy could both prevent the development of a revolutionary will among the general mass of the proletariat and establish that partial alliance between the manual workers and the lower-middle-class elements attached to large-scale capitalism which has been a marked feature of the evolution of Social Democracy.

It is, of course, possible to argue that Marx, whatever his errors and over-simplifications of secondary issues, was nevertheless fundamentally right in his verdict concerning the importance of the middle classes as a creative social force, when once the *grande bourgeoisie* had ceased to be their ally and had become itself the leading element in the upper class. That is a matter which it falls outside the scope of this paper to discuss. I am here concerned with Marxism solely from the standpoint of its influence on the conception of the 'middle class'. Wherever Marxism won acceptance, the middle class ceased to be looked upon as a coherent or creative social group, and came to be thought of as merely a nuisance getting in the way of the real historic conflict between the developed *grande bourgeoisie* and the proletariat—a decaying class to liquidate which, or any of its elements, was simply doing the work of history.

This notion of the middle classes seemed, in Great Britain, to be confirmed by the eclipse of the once great Liberal Party. If the signs were much less clear in France and Germany, the differences were usually put down to the less advanced stage reached by French capitalism and to the continued power in Germany of the old, feudal aristocratic classes, which still largely dominated the State. Before President Roosevelt's New Deal, the social situation in the United States appeared to lend itself fairly well to interpretation, of which the superficiality was not easily to be seen, in terms of a developing conflict between big business and the Trade Unions, with the rest of the people as little more than spectators. To-day, however, these readings of current history look much less plausible than they did before 1939, or even before 1945. In Western Europe, except in Great Britain and Scandinavia, the conflict between Communism and Social Democracy, by splitting the working class, has handed political power back to predominantly middle-class groups whose antagonism to Socialism ranges them with the *grande bourgeoisie*, but does not make them by any means entirely its servants. It may be said that this régime could not have been established, and could not survive, but for the powerful support given to it by the United States. That is probably true; but it does not alter the fact that, whatever the reasons, middle-class influence has been waxing and not waning in Western Europe, and has certainly not been extinguished in the United States, despite the very advanced stage of American capitalist development.

No doubt, the Marxian picture can be so re-drawn as to show us the world of to-day as dominated by two great powers, standing respectively for proletarian revolution and for imperialist capitalism, with all other countries in process of being reduced rapidly to the status of helpless satellites of the one or the other. That is how Communists do regard the world, looking upon the 'capitalist democracies' of the West as essentially 'middle-class' countries in process of being ground to powder between the two great contestants for world power. They may be right or wrong about this: I am not attempting to judge. If, however, it is the fate of Western Europe to be thus counted out as a force in history, this will not be because the internal evolution of the Western democracies has followed the Marxist pattern, but because they are too weak to stand up to external forces which have developed in different ways. Nor am I at all prepared to accept that interpretation of current history which treats the Soviet Union as the unquestionable exemplar of the workers' emancipation or the United States as the no less unquestionable embodiment of capitalist imperialism on the point of falling finally a victim to the 'contradictions of capitalism'. I cannot see either of them as the fulfilment of Marx's prophecies, according to which Russia was quite the wrong country to be the pioneer of Socialist revolution, and America ˌthe very country in which the middle classes ought by now to have been thoroughly snuffed out.

But, observe, Marx spoke usually not of the 'middle classes', but of the *bourgeoisie*, great or small. And this difference of terminology has an important bearing on the entire question which this paper sets out to discuss.

The phrase 'middle class' is often used as if it were simply the equivalent of the French *bourgeois* or of the German and other equivalents of that essentially *urban* designation. But in truth 'middle class' and *bourgeois* are not only different words, but stand for essentially different ideas. *Bourgeois*, to any historically-minded person, calls up at once the image of a body of citizens asserting their collective, as well as their individual, independence of a social system dominated by feudal power based on landholding and on the services attached to it; whereas the words 'middle class' call up the quite different image of a body of persons who are placed between two other bodies—or perhaps more than two—in some sort of stratified social order. The *bourgeois* is by his very name a claimant, not for himself alone but for a group with which he identifies his claim, to social power and recognition. He is one who claims, in common with the rest of his group, to be allowed to manage his affairs as suits best the way of life for which his group stands, instead of being subjected to a rule laid down for him by superiors whose values and needs differ fundamentally from those of which he has become conscious as a city-dweller, engaged in the traffic of trade and craftsmanship and seeking ever larger opportunities for the development of the mercantile and mechanic arts.

The 'middle class' conception is quite different from this. The *bourgeois*, as such, is not in the middle of anything—at any rate not consciously so. Looking back, we may be able to picture him, if we choose, as standing somehow between an aristocracy based on land and privilege and an unprivileged mass which included the great majority of the people. But this is not, historically, a legitimate way of looking at the *bourgeois* as he emerges into the light of the medieval record. It is altogether wrong either to lump together the main body of the urban workers and the peasants in the countryside as an unprivileged 'lower class' or to count the whole body of urban craftsmen as belonging to the *bourgeoisie* equally with the upper strata of gild masters and merchants, and as constituting, with these elements, a coherent 'middle class'. It is illegitimate to do either of these things because the very term 'middle class' implies being in the middle of some unitary structure that can be at least loosely defined. But the *bourgeoisie*, in its earlier phases of development, was not in the middle of anything that can be defined as a unitary structure. It came to be in the middle only later on, when, largely as the outcome of similar struggles in which it had played an ever-increasing part, cities ceased to be mainly *enclaves* in predominantly rural societies dominated by feudal institutions and came instead to be the predominant elements in societies in which industry, commerce, and the use of money and credit had become the main formative influences. Then, indeed, especially in capital cities and great centres of long-distance trade and exchange, the *bourgeoisie* came to be a middle class standing between the governing class—the aristocracy—on the one hand and the main body of citizens on the other; but this middle status still related mainly to their position in the towns. A revolution in the land system, bringing with it new forms of capitalist agriculture, was needed to create even a partly analogous situation in the rural areas, and to bring into existence a class of capitalist farmers who shared in some degree (though by no means completely) the culture and outlook of the urban *bourgeoisie*. But even where this rural revolution occurred, it did not necessarily carry with it an assimilation of urban and rural workers into a composite 'lower class'. Such assimilation occurred to the greatest extent only where what is called the 'domestic system' spread industrial production widely over the countryside, creating a large body of non-urban industrial workers actually or virtually in the employment of capitalist merchant-entrepreneurs. The more such a situation came about, the more the social differences between city and country became blurred, and whole areas came to be integrated into unitary economic and political systems. This, however, occurred only in exceptional cases, and never completely. Over a large part of Europe, though there was developed an urban *bourgeoisie*, there never did come into existence anything that can properly be called a 'middle class', at any rate not on a scale great enough to set its mark on the general course of social and political development. Where the *bourgeoisie* did not spread into the countryside, but remained as an urban *enclave* in a feudal society either developing towards a peasant economy or still dominated by great landed estates worked with serf, or quasi-serf, labour, there was no room for the evolution of a 'middle class' on a national scale, and none accordingly for the permeation of the whole society by the characteristically 'liberal' values which are associated chiefly with *bourgeois* development. This was the more so because in such societies the professional and intellectual classes developed largely as servants of the State, and thus became bureaucrats rather than 'liberals'.

This, of course, did not prevent individual members of the *bourgeoisie* in countries in which the town-dwellers remained essentially isolated from the countryside from regarding themselves as members of a 'middle class'. But, where they did so, they were still the victims of their isolation. They could not, like the *bourgeois* of the advancing capitalist countries, establish a pattern of life and then proceed to impress it upon the entire societies in which they lived: they could for the most part only copy the patterns and values that were being established by their compeers in the more capitalistic countries and pride themselves, on the strength of this, on being the pioneers of civilization *in partibus infidelium*; and the more they copied, and took pride in copying, the greater their isolation became. That is why 'liberalism' could never strike real roots over a large part of Europe: that is why there are no foundations to-day over a large part of Europe for political or economic systems which comply with the requirements of 'democracy', as democracy is understood in the Western countries that have experienced capitalistic unification. That, in effect, is why there is an 'iron curtain' in Europe, and why 'democracy' means so different things to Stalin and to Attlee or Churchill or Truman—for, however widely these three may differ in the meanings they attach to the word, they agree in meaning by it something that neither Stalin nor Tito can possibly either mean or even understand.

I think I have said enough in this paper to show that the concept of the middle class is exceedingly elusive, by whatever route one approaches it. Clearly, membership of the middle class, or classes, is not simply a matter of income, either absolutely or of relative income within a particular social structure. Nor is it exclusively a matter of the nature and source of the income received, or of profession or calling. Nor again is it exclusively a matter of education, or of manners; for no definition based on these will avail to mark off one part of the middle classes from the upper class or another from the working class. Nor will it serve to treat the family as a unit; for it is nowadays very common for one child from a working-class household to enter a profession, while another becomes a manual worker, and yet another marries a local shopkeeper, after a spell of either factory or clerical employment. In modern fluid societies, the family ceases in more and more instances to be a unit assignable to a single class. This, of course, is not new, for priesthoods have usually been recruited from a wide variety of social groups; but it is commoner now than ever before, except in pioneering societies such as the United States and the British Dominions, not only for the family to be made up of varying class elements, but also for individuals to shift from class to class on their way through life. This does not mean that classes lose reality; but it does mean that their boundaries become more and more difficult to draw.

I can perhaps best end with a very rough attempt to designate the main groups of which the 'middle classes' can be regarded as made up to-day in Great Britain and, I think, also in most of the more advanced countries of the West. Of course, the proportions in which these various elements are found differ widely from country to country, and there are also considerable differences of relative status and of relations to other sections of the population. Subject to these qualifications, I put forward the following very tentative classification of groups:

(a) The main body of heads of private businesses, or of active partners or directors in businesses, except the greatest, concerned with manufacture or wholesale trading, or with other commercial or financial occupations.

(b) The main body of salaried administrators, managers, technicians, and accountants in similar types of business, including businesses publicly or co-operatively owned; and the higher salaried officers of a wide range of institutions and societies, from political parties and Trade Unions or Trade Associations to philanthropic, educational, and cultural bodies.

(c) The members of the principal recognized professions, whether salaried or working as consultants and remunerated by professional fees; including medical men, lawyers, ministers of religion, officers of the armed services, the upper ranges of the teaching profession, and the upper and middle ranges of the artistic and industrial professions.

(*d*) The higher and middle grades of the Civil Service, the Local Government service, and of other public or semi-public administrative services; and the corresponding grades of 'voluntary' social service employees.

(*e*) The big and middle shopkeepers, garage keepers, hotel keepers; and also the analogous groups of employed managers, accountants, and other officers employed by joint stock companies operating in these fields.

(*f*) The large and middle farmers: and with them the relatively small numbers of managerial salaried workers employed on big farms.

(*g*) The unoccupied *rentiers*, living on unearned incomes, except the largest and some of the smallest—the latter a group composed mainly of retired persons, widows, poor relations of wealthy families, reduced members of the aristocracy, and other very heterogeneous minor groups.

(*h*) Full-time students who have embarked on higher education at a university or comparable level, but have not completed their education, including students drawn from working-class households.

(*i*) More doubtfully, the main bodies of clerks, typists, and other non-manual workers whose work falls below the managerial or recognized professional level.

(*j*) Still more doubtfully, the members of certain lesser professions, such as nursing, the lower ranges of school teaching, and the less recognized social service occupations.

(*k*) Most doubtfully of all, the main body of shop assistants, warehouse workers, postal workers other than clerks, and minor institutional officials.

(*l*) Just possibly, persons belonging to the lower supervisory grades in industry, transport, and other types of business, but falling below the managerial grades.

How far is there anything in common among these very diverse groups, beyond their lying in some sense between the upper classes—the very rich and the born aristocrats—and the main body of manual wage-workers? They include the great majority of those who receive more than a very small part of their incomes in the form of either interest or profits; but they also include a large and ever-increasing proportion whose main income is derived from salaries, and salaries at the lower levels are barely distinguishable from wages, which are the characteristic incomes of the working classes. Many of the lower salaries, but also some of the higher, are negotiated by methods of collective bargaining closely akin to trade union wage-negotiations, and, in Great Britain at any rate, there is a growing tendency for the lesser salary-earners to join the Trades Union Congress and to regard themselves as belonging with, and in many cases to, the working-class movement. Not only the shop assistant and the clerk, but also to an increasing extent the scientific worker, the supervisor, and the civil servant, except at the highest levels, are on the whole aligned with the manual workers against the profit-makers and the *rentiers*, when it comes to a question of the distribution of the national income or the development of the social services and of the 'welfare State'. The *intelligentsia*, centred mainly on the upper professions, does no doubt form a recognizable and essentially middle-class group; but its unity is much more of culture and manners than of economic interest or social and political attitude, and it forms only a fraction of the middle class, even on the narrowest definition. It has less in common culturally with most farmers, shopkeepers, or small employers than these have with the main body of skilled manual workers, or than it has itself with workers who have imbibed its culture through adult education or home influence. Yet it can be said, with truth and with very practical implications, that a very large proportion of the heterogeneous groups that make up the middle classes have a common concern with the defence of economic and social inequality against levelling tendencies which threaten either their incomes or their property or those parts of the social structure which narrow the ways of entry into the better-paid occupations and thus keep down the competition for superior jobs. This, when it comes to the point, is their chief common interest; for the defence of culture and of the higher liberal values is the concern only of a fraction of the middle classes, and that by no means the most influential fraction when they attempt to act together as a class.

What future lies before this ill-defined, heterogeneous 'middle class' that can be labelled as a class only because the groups that make it up can be identified neither with the aristocracy and *grande bourgeoisie* nor with the wage-earners? Certainly, except in the countries which have passed under Communist domination, it shows no sign of disappearing. It is not, as Marx prophesied, being driven down into the proletariat by the development of capitalism: on the contrary, advancing capitalism has shown itself exceedingly favourable to its multiplication, and declining capitalism, where we have examples of it, seems to drive the middle groups towards Fascism rather than towards an acceptance of the status of proletarians. The evidence for this may be discounted on the ground that it is drawn from countries in which there had been no real decline of capitalism but only an undermining of the middle classes by war and inflation, and that Fascism is to be regarded as a product of these forces rather than of any internal evolution of capitalism itself. The Communist will answer that war and inflation are themselves portents of capitalist contradictions, and that wars have merely hastened and accentuated the tendencies inherent in the capitalist system. The fact remains that neither in Great Britain nor in the United States has anything that can properly be called Fascism as yet assumed dangerous proportions, or the position of the middle classes been fundamentally undermined.

There is, no doubt, an important difference in this respect between Great Britain and the United States, in that capitalism itself has been seriously challenged in the one country, but not in the other. In America, capitalism, though it has been forced to make substantial concessions to the claims of Labour and to the 'Welfare State', is still an advancing system, carrying along with it a prosperous middle income group into which more and more of the superior wage-earners have been able to climb. In Great Britain, on the other hand, capitalism, under pressure from the poorer sections of the population, has been forced to give ground by submitting to

97

levels of taxation that have considerably reduced inequalities of spendable income, though not of capital ownership. But, as against this narrowing of the gulf between the extremes, the process of increasing the size of the middle groups has gone on uninterrupted, and the salary differentials characteristic of big business have been carried over into the administrative structure of the newly nationalized industries. Certainly the development of the Welfare State in Great Britain has not, in raising the living standards of the worst-off, thrown down the professional and managerial groups into the ranks of the proletariat or ground down shopkeepers and farmers into the mass of the unprivileged. On the contrary, it has made large concessions to the claims of doctors, shopkeepers, farmers, and small business men, giving them both bigger incomes and greater security than they have ever before enjoyed. It is true that some groups usually ranked as 'middle class' have fared relatively ill—for example, Civil Servants, teachers, and local government officers, as well as small *rentiers* dependent on fixed money incomes. But there has been no sign of an impending *écrasement* of the middle class as a whole: rather, a growth of some of its groups compensating for a decline of others, and resulting in a change in its composition and social stratification.

Nor has the supersession of capitalism by proletarian revolution crushed out the middle groups, even in the Soviet Union. One is not allowed to speak of 'classes' as existing, save as survivals, in Communist-dominated society; but no one denies the persistence of large differences of income and social prestige, or the existence of a marked tendency towards increasing differentiation, in the Stalinist epoch of Soviet development.

Some writers have gone so far as to claim that these tendencies are signs of the inevitable advent of what James Burnham has dubbed a 'managerial revolution' and proclaimed as a necessary product of the evolution of the 'powers of production', irrespective of differences of political régime. For my part, I find such notions confusing and grossly oversimplified. If all that is meant is that the development of modern techniques of mass-production and large-scale administration necessarily requires the existence of a large body of highly trained scientists, technicians, administrators and managers, who are bound to claim, for a long time to come, superior rewards and a superior status in society by virtue of their natural or acquired qualities of usefulness, there is nothing to argue about; for no one in his senses is likely to dispute the fact. If, however, it is argued that these occupants of superior positions are bound to become the real masters of society, however it may be nominally governed in its political affairs, I not merely dissent, but see no basis for the contention that does not rest on a sheer confusion of terms. James Burnham, in his much publicized book, *The Managerial Revolution*, supported his argument by shifting at caprice from one definition of his terms to another, treating as 'the managers' now the great capitalist entrepreneurs and now the large body of technicians and managerial employees, just as happened to suit his case. Moreover, he resorted to a facile identification of this ill-defined 'class' in capitalist countries with the privileged 'managers' under the Soviet system, though such evidence as there is goes to show rather separateness than unity between the privileged income groups in the Soviet economic system and the governing party *élite*.

Indeed, I can come no nearer to a conclusion about the future of the 'middle classes' than to say that a study of the recent evolution in both capitalist and Soviet countries goes to show, mainly, two things—first, that the road to economic equality, even if open, is much longer and more difficult than many Socialists used to suppose, and that the mere supersession of capitalism by a sort of Socialism by no means wipes out differences of income or of social status, though it does, as Marx long ago said it would, largely substitute income differences based on personal service and capacity for differences based on ownership of property or of inherited economic claims. Secondly, that, as economic differences come to be more closely related to personal capacities and educational advantages, and as education and training come to be more and more state-provided services open to wider sections of the population, social and economic superiority come, in

99

capitalist as well as in socialist countries, to be more individual, and much less family, matters and thus lose a substantial part of their old, undemocratic character. For, after
all, the conception of class is, historically, related very inti-
mately to that of family status, not only for landed aristocracies but also for the social groups which base their claims
on commerce or industry, or on monopoly, or near-monopoly,
of the 'gentlemanly' professions. Where the family loses its
class character under the influence either of abundant
economic opportunity or of an open educational system resting on public provision at the higher as well as at the lower
levels, 'middle class' tends to become a merely descriptive
adjective, designating those in the middle, rather than a term
defining a distinctive section of the population. A 'middle
class' may still be held to exist under such conditions—that
is really a matter of words—but a *bourgeoisie*, in the sense
historically attaching to the term, cannot.

V

Élites in British Society

I. INTRODUCTORY

WHO really governs Great Britain to-day—in 1955? The 'Government', in the narrowest sense of the term, has been for four years in the hands of the leaders of a single political party—the Conservative Party— and before that was for six years in the hands of its principal rival—the Labour Party. Before that, it had been for five years in the hands of a wartime Coalition, with a Conservative Prime Minister, but with the leading members of the Labour Party occupying the key economic positions in home affairs. Before that, again, it had been in the hands of the Conservative Party, and before that of a 'National' Government in which the Conservatives held a clear preponderance over other parties. Before that ... but what profits it to go back through the record of successive one-party or coalition Governments? For assuredly, in the sense which concerns us in this study, not one of these Governments 'governed' Great Britain in any exclusive sense. They were no more than the highest executive authority in a structure of government of which they formed only a part— and not even, from the standpoint of the political theorist, the sociologist, or the historian, necessarily the most important part.

Take, then, the word 'government' in a rather wider sense, to include the legislature as well as the executive. Great Britain lives under a theoretically unlimited system of 'Parliamentary Government'. There is, in theory, no limit to what the British Parliament—made up of King, Lords, and Commons—can do. There is no written constitution, no formal safeguard against the exercise of parliamentary power. Parliament is free, in theory, to pass what laws it

STUDIES IN CLASS STRUCTURE

pleases and to set up what authorities it pleases to administer its laws. The judges, individually and collectively, are without any constitutional power to stand out against, or to disallow, anything Parliament makes law. They can interpret the law, including not only Statute Law but also Common Law, which is not created by statute; but they can do this only subject to the power of Parliament to make and order the execution of statutes which override the Common Law. Parliament is 'sovereign', if that much-abused word means anything: it has made a king, and it could abolish the monarchy—though constitutionally only with the Crown's consent, for the Crown is a part of Parliament, and no Bill can become an Act unless the Crown accepts it. But we are still moving, plainly, in a realm of unrealities, or of half-realities at best; for Parliament, no more than the executive Government, can claim in fact to 'govern' Great Britain in any exclusive sense.

The subject of this study is not, save quite incidentally, the formal constitutional structure of government in Great Britain, but the actual disposition of political and social forces that determines the conditions within which Governments, in the narrower sense, govern, within which Parliament makes the laws and in some degree watches over their administration, and within which the entire complex structure of social life works. In particular, we are setting out to enquire into the nature of the directing influences and groups which, by their conflicts and agreements and by their very assumptions, limit the effective powers of Parliaments and Governments, and of much besides, and shape the course of British political and social life.

In the parlance of continental thought, these directing influences and groups are commonly called *élites*—a word for which, significantly, no English equivalent has been found. We do not speak, in Great Britain, of the 'chosen' or, since the seventeenth century, transfer to secular affairs the theological concept of the 'elect'. The term *élite*, if I mistake not, was first used in Great Britain in an entirely non-political sense, to designate those who had the assured entry to 'High Society'—a grouping in which it was the fashion to make use of a sprinkling of French words for expressing aristocratic values. The *élite*, in this sense, was what Englishmen more often called the 'nobs', the 'toffs', the 'upper ten', or the 'aristocracy'. No doubt the aristocracy was, at the time when this usage prevailed, an exceedingly powerful and influential political and social force; but the name had reference, not to this aspect of it, but rather to its assumption of superiority and exclusiveness in the field of personal relations. When continental sociologists began to speak of *élites* in a much wider sense, of which aristocracies were no more than an instance, and when Englishmen had to translate the new concept into English, no English word was found for it, and the French word slipped into the technical language of Politics and Sociology just as it was slipping out of use in its older, 'high society', sense. It has never become truly naturalized in this second usage: there is still, for any Englishman who uses the term, a sense of applying a foreign concept to a British situation. English-speakers have never quite fully naturalized that convenient word '*bourgeois*', despite the Marxists: it will take a great deal to make us either fully absorb, or find an English equivalent for, the word '*élite*'.

Indeed, many of us do not like the word, because we are not at all sure what precisely it is intended to mean. It can be used to mean so many different things. Is it, for example, meant to be essentially a *class* designation, to be used to indicate some group, or groups, that holds a position of influence at the top level of a society and controls, or plays an important part in controlling, the affairs of the entire society from its point of vantage? This is, I think, the sense in which Pareto usually employed the term. In this sense, one could speak of 'Big Business' in the United States, or the Communist Party leadership in the Soviet Union, or the upper strata of the church hierarchy in Spain, or of the military hierarchy in Japan up to 1945, as constituting an *élite* in some respects comparable with the 'nobility' of past days in Western Europe. But there is a vital difference, of which we must not lose sight. The old aristocracies, even if they were to varying extents open in practice to social climbers, were essentially hereditary in their basis. Most of their members were born into them, and belonged to them as of right, irrespective of personal qualities. But all these other ruling groups, even if heredity has some influence on their recruitment, are in essence constituted on a basis of some sort of personal capacity, and individuals can drop out of them as a result of personal failure, as well as rise into them as a reward for success. If such *élites* lead society, they do so because they have become possessed of some influential power in society, and not merely because they have been born into the exercise of such a power.

Those who set out to use the word *élite* as a class designation often appear to be in a considerable state of uncertainty about what they really mean. For example, if 'Big Business' is called an *élite*, does the word apply to the entire body of persons who are engaged in large-scale business either as entrepreneurs or as salaried administrators, or only to those who have risen to the highest levels of the business hierarchy and are big owners of capital as well as powerful administrators of affairs? The two notions are essentially different, the one depending on an attachment to a particular power-structure, and the other on the personal possession both of wealth and of high administrative authority within that structure. Or again, do those who speak of the Communist Party of the Soviet Union as an *élite* mean to include the entire membership of the party, or only those members who exercise substantial influence within it; and, if the latter, influence at what levels? Yet again, does the *élite* of the Catholic Church include the village priest, or only those members of the hierarchy who exercise influence at higher levels? The whole conception of the *élite* as a class, clearly applicable to hereditary aristocracies, becomes much more elusive when the attempt is made to apply it to groups which do not rest on a basis of heredity or carry their relatives with them, and may recruit their members from wide bodies of persons who, until they have personally achieved promotion, cannot at all be regarded as belonging to the same group as those who have obviously climbed up into positions of leadership.

I find this confusion pervading Mr. James Burnham's account of the managerial class in his often-quoted book,

The Managerial Revolution. Sometimes, he seems to be speaking only of the limited group of big financiers, capitalists, and administrators in whose hands the direction of large-scale business is concentrated. At other times, he appears to be thinking mainly of the possessors of high technological capacity, as distinct from the mere capital-owners. At yet other times, he appears to be including the general mass of shareholders, even if they are neither technically qualified nor active as administrators or directors of business policy. To the extent to which I can attach meaning to his speculations, he seems to have in mind, as Saint Simon had a century and a half before him, the plain fact that the development of technology, based on the advance of science, tends to confer power and prestige on the possessors of technical and business competence, as against the politicians and the aristocrats, whose education has tended to rest on a foundation of law and classical or philosophic culture. This is true enough; but it does not carry us far until we know the social mechanisms through which the new scientific education can be acquired, the extent to which its acquisition is open to persons of widely different social origins, and the ways in which those who gain the requisite knowledge are able to climb up to the higher levels of the economic and social hierarchy. It is one thing to say that, in a world dominated by the effects of scientific discovery, more of the key positions of power are bound to be occupied by persons who understand the potentialities of applied science: it is quite another thing to maintain that in such a world the possessors of this understanding are bound to develop into a ruling class. This latter assertion involves the familiar fallacy of the distributed middle—some men are technically qualified: some technically qualified persons climb to high positions of power: therefore all technically qualified persons form an *élite.* The conclusion does not follow from the premises: even if *all* possessors of high power needed to be technically qualified —which they do not—it would not by any means follow that all technically qualified persons were members of an *élite.*

In this chapter, I propose to consider *élites,* not as constituting social classes, but rather as groups which emerge to positions of leadership and influence *at every social level*—that is to say, as leaders of classes or of other important elements in the social structure. I am here using the word 'leader' in a wide sense, to designate not only *Fuehrers* or officially appointed chiefs but also all persons who, for whatever reason, exercise a substantial influence on the social attitudes and social conduct of any considerable section of the groups to which they are attached. In this sense, the more active and influential members of a church congregation, or of a Trade Union, or of a body of employees working together as a productive team, of a Co-operative Society or a political party nationally or locally, or of a propagandist association, or of a voluntary body engaged in 'Social Service'—all these, and many others, constitute more or less important *élites* in relation to the particular groups they are connected with—and in many cases over a much wider field.

The social theorist cannot, however, rest content with merely cataloguing these numerous *élites*: he must seek in addition to assess their several degrees of importance in any particular community as a whole. He needs to study not only the degree of influence exercised by each *élite* over the group through which it emerges, but also the influence which these groups, guided by their several *élites*, have on social behaviour over a wider field, and on the entire pattern of community life. Accordingly, in repudiating the identification of the *élite* with a 'ruling class', he cannot discard altogether the need to pay attention to the *rôle* of certain *élites* as leaders of classes and exponents of class attitudes, as promoters of 'class consciousness', and as opponents of the claims of rival classes. Not all *élites* rest on a class basis, or are to be regarded as class representatives; but some do and are, and a special importance attaches, in modern societies and especially in the older societies which have been developing from aristocracy towards some form of democracy, to the relations between classes and *élites* and to the differences that emerge with the increasing complexities of class structure.

Elsewhere, I have described the present class structure of Great Britain as consisting of three separate systems, of which the second and third have been in turn superimposed on the first, in such a way as to leave all three still in existence, but with their relative importance greatly changed. These three are, first, an old structure based on relations to the land, and essentially aristocratic in character; secondly, a predominantly plutocratic structure based on the development of modern commerce and industry; and thirdly a much more diversified structure based on the growth of professional and administrative work, and closely affected by the wider diffusion and considerably differentiated development of the educational system. This very broad characterization of the three historical elements in the British class structure of to-day may be of some help as a clue to the understanding of the selection and arrangement of the materials used in this essay.

Using the term *élites* in the very wide sense I have indicated, I cannot within the limited space at my disposal mention more than a very few of the immense number of *élites* which, in one way or another, make their impact on the pattern of community behaviour, or attempt to indicate how more than a very few of them have grown up. I think I am most likely to make good use of my space if I begin, not with the directly economic phenomena of class divisions by occupational or income groups, but rather with the latest of the three 'systems'—the educational.

II. THE EDUCATIONAL FACTORS

Anyone who sets out to understand the social structure of Great Britain to-day must begin by paying close attention to the educational system. This system—if system is the right word for it—can be understood only in the light of its historical development during the nineteenth and twentieth centuries. In the eighteenth century, broadly speaking, there were three quite distinct kinds of formal education, and side by side with them a fourth, the learning of a skilled trade by formal or informal apprenticeship. For the poor, including the great mass of the people, there were parish schools, 'dame' schools, Charity Schools supported by the contributions of the wealthy. All these agencies together fell a long way short of reaching the whole of the children for whom they were designed; but they represented a kind of schooling devised explicitly for members of the lower classes. The main ladder leading out of these schools to a higher social status was that of apprenticeship to a skilled trade; and those who were able to climb this ladder were raised a considerable height above the mere 'labourers', and had some chance of climbing further into the ranks of the small masters who still dominated most of the industrial crafts. At the other end of the social scale, there was a structure of aristocratic education, based partly on a few privileged schools but to a much greater extent on the employment of private tutors in the households of wealthy men, or in the case of the lesser squirearchy and gentlefolk on reading with clergymen who took a few private pupils. At the highest levels, foreign travel, with a tutor in attendance, played a large part in the final stages of the educational process; but the general run of 'gentlemen' could not afford such luxuries, and had to keep their sons at home. The education of women of the upper classes was mainly in the hands of tutors and governesses: if they went abroad, it was *en famille*, when the household made a continental tour, or to visit relatives domiciled overseas. The upper-class seminary for girls was indeed already making its appearance; but it was chiefly for the daughters of West Indian planters or Indian nabobs, who sent their children home to school, or for those of non-aristocratic wealthy families intent on equipping their daughters with the refinements needed for social climbing.

Between these two educational structures there was a third, developing rapidly with the growth of commercial and industrial wealth. The Nonconformist Academies, set up in the first instance mainly for the training of recruits for the ministries of the various Dissenting sects, played an important part in the evolution of this intermediate system. Many sons of well-to-do Dissenters were sent to these Academies not as a preparation for the ministry but because they offered the best higher education available for those who were outside the Established Church, as a large proportion of the successful merchants and industrialists were, and wished their children to be. Side by side with these Academies there developed, as the century advanced, many private schools which held out the promise of a sound commercial education at a price within the means of middle-class parents who could not afford to send their sons away to board, or did not wish to. These Commercial Academies became the rivals of the older Grammar Schools, which were in many cases in a state of decay, but, where they were active, mostly provided a narrowly classical education under the control of Churchmen. In the first quarter of the nineteenth century there was a considerable revival of the Grammar Schools, without much modification of the old classical curricula or of the Church control over their affairs. The revival, however, brought into them a large number of the sons of local tradesmen and small employers, as well as of the rapidly increasing professional classes. Often, in the first half of the nineteenth century, a town had both a Grammar School and one or more Commercial Academies, the former carrying the higher social prestige, but seldom rising to the privilege of educating members of the upper class.

At this point came the major educational development that is usually associated with the name of Dr. Thomas Arnold of Rugby, the father of Matthew Arnold. Dr. Arnold transformed Rugby from a local Grammar School into a 'public school' of an essentially new type, designed to provide boarding education above all for the sons of the higher grades of professional men, and with them for such sons of the wealthier men of business as their fathers could be induced to trust to his care. Arnold was a classical scholar, a Churchman, and an ardent believer in the need to civilize the rising middle classes. The type of school which he set out to create was meant, not to be a higher kind of Commercial Academy, but to make Christian gentlemen with a taste for literary culture, but also with a strong sense of social responsibility and a high code of moral conduct. Arnold's Rugby was a part of the challenge of Liberal Churchmanship to Nonconformity, as well as an attempt to turn as many as possible of the sons of the new wealthy into men of culture and inheritors of the old traditions of aristocratic learning and manners.

Dr. Arnold, and other less celebrated headmasters who worked along similar lines, had an enormous influence on the development of middle-class education in the second half of the nineteenth century. The English 'public school' system, as it exists to-day, is mainly of their making: it embraces old foundations, such as Eton and Winchester, transformed Grammar Schools turned into boarding schools with a national standing, such as Rugby, and a great number of new foundations modelled upon these examples. On the fringe of the system are certain great day schools, such as St. Paul's in London and Manchester Grammar School, which provide much the same kind of education, but are sometimes distinguished from 'public schools' in the full sense because boarding education is regarded as essential to the 'public school' idea. Outside observers are sometimes puzzled to find these schools called 'public', when they are entirely independent of the State and essentially separate from the general system of education under public control. They came to be called 'public schools' in order to distinguish them from private schools carried on for profit, their distinguishing character being that they are conducted under public trusts or charters, with independent Boards of Governors who have no financial interest in them. These 'public schools' became, in the course of the nineteenth century, the principal training ground both for aristocrats and plutocrats, as the practice of employing private tutors gradually lapsed, and also for the children of the upper business and professional classes, especially for those who were intended to enter a profession requiring higher education. They became the main source of recruits for the Universities, and their *alumni* provided the main body of entrants into the higher ranks of the Civil Service, as well as to the Church, to the barrister section of the law, and then, more gradually, to medicine and to the higher ranks of the scientific professions. They were, however, late in the field in paying adequate attention to science, and retained, until well on into the twentieth century, a strong classical bias, which has not even now at all completely disappeared.

The English 'public school', then, came to occupy the key position in the selection of those who were to fill the positions of influence over a very wide field. At this stage, the State played no part at all in either providing or controlling higher education, beyond appointing two Royal Commissions which enquired into the working and endowments of the older 'public schools' in the 1860s. The State, indeed, did not seriously enter into the field of higher education until after 1918, under the 'Fisher' Act, though a small beginning had been made under powers conferred by the 'Balfour' Education Act of 1902. The system of education under State auspices introduced by the 'Forster' Education Act of 1870 was meant to be confined to elementary schooling for the children of the poor, and was not designed to cater for the needs of the children of the even moderately well-to-do at any age. In practice, some local School Boards soon strained the meaning of the Act by setting out to provide schooling at somewhat higher levels, both in 'higher grade' junior schools and in what came to be called 'Central Schools' for some of the more advanced older children. In 1899 a famous decision, the 'Cockerton' Judgment, declared certain of these practices to lie beyond the powers conferred by the Education Acts, and it was one of the purposes of the Act of 1902 to amend the law in this respect. But even after 1902 the general assumption was that state provision of higher education would for the most part stop at an intermediate level and would not be at any point competitive with the provisions made in the 'public schools' and in the growing number of preparatory schools that were being set up to prepare the children of the well-to-do for entry to the 'public schools'. Nor was state-provided education meant to compete with the local Grammar Schools, but rather to send on to them such of its scholars as seemed suitable for the more literary forms of secondary schooling. Right up to the 1920s only a few boys of more than fifteen years of age were being educated in state schools, and only a few were staying on at most of the Grammar Schools much beyond sixteen, though a few of the major Grammar Schools in the big cities kept a high proportion of their pupils up to eighteen, and sent a considerable number of them on to a University.

Up to this point, as far as boys were concerned, there were four main streams of entrants to 'gainful employment', or, in a limited number of cases, to the life of a 'gentleman' living on his private means. At the lower end there was the broad stream of children leaving school at fourteen or earlier, and entering immediately upon some sort of paid work. Some of these would become apprenticed to skilled trades, and some, by attending 'night schools', would later pick up some special vocational qualification. But most of them would go into industry or commerce as juvenile workers, or at most as 'learners' without formal apprenticeship.

The second main stream, leaving school at fifteen or sixteen, would flow largely into routine clerical employment, but would include a considerable number of boys taken into family businesses, or found business positions by private influence, mostly in relatively small-scale enterprises. This stream would flow partly out of the Central Schools set up under the Education Acts, partly out of the Grammar Schools, and partly out of private-venture secondary schools conducted for profit, and not subject to any form of public supervision. From this second main stream would diverge several subsidiary streams—notably, those proceeding to a two-year course of training to be teachers in elementary schools, and a few passing on to full-time training in a local Technical College. This last group, however, was very small, as most technical education remained on a part-time basis of 'evening school' work combined with 'gainful employment'.

The third main stream consisted of those who stayed on at a 'public school', or at a superior Grammar School, until eighteen or nineteen, and then went into business without proceeding to a University or College. This stream included many entrants to family businesses, and also 'premium apprentices' sent to big firms to be trained for managerial positions.

The fourth, and highest, stream, after staying at a superior school to eighteen or nineteen, went on to the University stage. But the character of this fourth stream changed—

and to some extent it became for a time two separate streams, with the great development of the newer Universities during the last decades of the nineteenth and, still more, the early decades of the twentieth century. The growth of these 'civic' Universities in most of the great cities made it a great deal easier for parents to give their clever children a university education and, in doing so, rendered it possible for the Grammar Schools and some of the lesser 'public schools' to keep a higher proportion of their pupils up to seventeen or eighteen, and then pass them on to the University. The biggest bodies of such new recruits to university education were on the one hand schoolmasters, who were needed in increasing numbers by the growing secondary schools, and on the other scientists and applied scientists, for whom there was coming to be a considerable demand from certain industries, notably chemicals and engineering. The newer Universities, which grew in some cases out of Technical Colleges catering mainly for evening students, were from the first active in the fields of science and higher technology; and at the same time there was a growing tendency for fathers whose sons were destined to 'business' careers as employers or managers to keep them longer at school, though not, in most cases, to send them on to a University. Thus, at a level somewhat lower in terms of social prestige than that of the older Universities, there flowed out from the new Universities as well as from the top forms of superior secondary schools a widening stream of recruits to business and to the middle ranges of professional life; whereas the higher professions still kept for some time longer their close relation to the old Universities or to certain more specialized providers of high education, such as the great teaching hospitals and the Architects' and other professional Institutes.

I have written so far mainly in terms of boys; but of course there were also, from the middle of the nineteenth century, great developments in the higher education of women. In their case there were no ancient institutions corresponding to the older 'public schools'; but there had come to be a large number of private-venture schools for boarders as well as for day-girls, devoted mainly to the teaching of accomplishments deemed suitable for 'young ladies', or for aspirants to that status. The parish and charity schools, the 'dame' schools, and the new schools set up during the first half of the nineteenth century under the 'monitorial' system provided for boys and girls together, though the subjects taught differed to some extent. Girls were taught 'domestic' subjects, especially needlework, and in many of the charity schools and other parish schools it was a primary object to produce a supply of girls suitable for domestic service. There did not, however, grow up in the case of women any form of intermediate provision such as was made for boys in the increasing number of Commercial Academies. When the revolt began against the superior girls' schools' excessive attention to ladylike accomplishments and to 'deportment' as against useful learning, the protagonists were mainly women drawn from the professional classes and in many cases active also in the wider struggle for 'Women's Rights'. The Christian Socialists, in the 1840s, headed by Frederick Maurice, were energetic pioneers in the cause of women's higher education; but the main impetus came a little later, though the Christian Socialist Queen's College of 1848 was swiftly followed by the establishment of Bedford College in 1849—now part of London University—and of Cheltenham Ladies' College—the pioneer high-class girls' boarding school—in 1855. The first and last of these were in effect 'public schools' for young ladies: the second, Bedford College, was the pioneer women's institution of university standard. Girton College began in 1869, and soon moved to Cambridge from its original home at Hitchin; and a national movement to establish a chain of 'public' high schools for girls was founded in 1872. This developed chiefly as an agency for setting up day schools rather than boarding schools; and the schools themselves were for the most part more like local Grammar Schools than like the traditional boys' 'public schools'. But there was also a growth of other girls' boarding schools, deliberately modelled on the 'public schools' for boys, and also of private-venture upper- and middle-class girls' schools, both for boarders and for day pupils. The effect of these developments was to supersede or largely to transform the 'Ladies' Seminaries, of the type already described, and to give a strong impetus to the entry of women, not only into the higher professions, but also into clerical and other types of employment. With them went a rapid growth of women's university education as the newer Universities grew up on a basis of equal accessibility to both sexes.

In relation to higher education generally the course of development in Scotland differed substantially from that in England. Scotland has only a very few schools at all analogous to the English 'public schools'; and the foundations of its educational system rest on parish schools which are attended by most of the population irrespective of social or economic class, complemented by urban 'academies' and grammar schools which provide secondary education without boarding for most scholars who remain at school beyond the minimum leaving age. Access to the Universities from the upper ranges of the school system has been much easier economically in Scotland than in England, largely because of an extensive system of grants financed by Andrew Carnegie's beneficence. The Scottish Universities, except St. Andrews, which is the smallest, have been for a long time past much more like the newer civic Universities in England than like Oxford and Cambridge, and have drawn their students from a wider social field. The development of the newer Universities in England, and also the growth of state-aided higher education in grammar schools and state secondary schools has greatly narrowed the differences between the two systems; but the absence of any substantial number of 'public schools' for boarders, drawing their pupils from a limited class of wealthy and professional families, still remains an outstanding point of contrast.

I have described the development of the British educational system at such length (and yet with too much compression to give more than the barest idea of its working) because it has been so vital a factor in the selection of those who have occupied the key positions at the different social levels. Of course, the schools and Universities could not have developed as they did had there not been economic forces favouring their forms of growth. But the new economic forces did not by themselves determine the shape taken by the educational system: they acted rather to modify a pre-existing structure of which the changes were also influenced by other forces of a non-economic character. For example, religious influences played a continuous part in shaping educational institutions; and the aristocratic, but not closed aristocratic, structure upon which the new economic forces made their impact was never completely broken by them; it not only survived in modified form, but also made its influence strongly felt in the development of the new institutions created to meet needs arising out of economic change.

III. THE RELIGIOUS FACTORS

Consider for a moment the influence of the religious factor. It is generally agreed that the dispute between Churchmen and Dissenters delayed for a long time the full assumption by the State of the responsibility for universalizing elementary education. But it did much more than this: it prevented the State from entering seriously into the field of higher education until well on into the twentieth century, and it was partly responsible for keeping the State right out of the field of university education for still longer. In the first half of the nineteenth century, the advanced educational reformers who were religious Dissenters were for the most part intensely hostile to state intervention because they thought it would involve control by the Established Church. Most of them reconciled themselves to the acceptance of state grants, given both to Church schools and to Dissenting or undenominational schools, because they realized the sheer impossibility of raising sufficient funds privately; but they remained exceedingly jealous of their independence and fearful of any extension of public control. As against this, many Churchmen believed that the Church ought to have full control over education and deeply hated the necessity of granting public money in aid of Dissenters' schools. It took many decades of accumulating need to persuade a

Government to recognize that it was necessary for the
State to step in and provide schools where neither Church
nor Dissenting agencies were doing the job on an adequate
scale to ensure every child a school place; and when at last,
in 1870, the Forster Act became law, the rights of both
Churchmen and Dissenters—and also of Roman Catholics—
to maintain their own schools, with aid from public funds,
had to be recognized not merely as the exception but as the
rule—state provision being limited to filling up the gaps.
This hybrid system, though the balance has shifted continuously towards the state schools, remains in being to-day,
having survived the Education Act of 1944. Most urban
schools are now publicly provided, except in strongly Roman
Catholic areas; but a high proportion of village schools
remains under Church control, though nowadays by far the
greater part of their cost is met from public funds.

Having to share control with the Dissenters in the field of
elementary education, Churchmen were determined to hold
on firmly to their control of higher education. The old
'public schools' and Grammar Schools were in nearly all
cases linked by their charters and constitutions to the
Established Church, and most of their headmasters were
clergymen. Their independent Governing Bodies consisted
of Churchmen, and Dissenters were for a long time rigidly
kept out. The older Universities were still more closely linked
to the Church: Oxford and Cambridge were closed to
Dissenters until 1871, and full equality was reached only by
stages over a long subsequent period. London University,
or rather University College, London, founded in 1826, was
from the first free from doctrinal tests; but it remained exceptional until the new Universities began to grow up in the
great provincial towns. Until the final quarter of the nineteenth century Churchmen had something approaching a
monopoly—not extending, of course, to Scotland—of the
highest ranges of education according to current ideas. Most
of the new 'public schools' which were founded to provide
for the higher education of the middle classes were con-
trolled by Churchmen: many a wealthy Dissenter had to
choose between having his children educated in a school

which took it for granted that 'gentlemen' ought to belong to the Established Church and accepting forms of schooling which were often of inferior quality and always carried a lower social prestige. The local Grammar Schools could not in practice keep out the Dissenters' children, but they could accept them while refusing to modify the Church basis of the schools. Gradually, however, the sheer weight of well-to-do Nonconformity affected the practice of these schools, relegating religious teaching to a minor place. The 'public' girls' schools grew up only at a time when the exclusive Church control was already breaking down, and were mostly able to start on a basis of greater religious equality; but, by contrast, many of the privately conducted higher girls' schools retained their church character in an accentuated form.

In England, the distinction between 'Church' and 'Chapel' has always, since the rise of Dissent, been a social as well as a religious distinction, both cutting across class differences and powerfully influencing estimations of class. The distinction is now less important than in the past; but it still exists, and it remained highly significant until a very little while ago. In many of the higher positions in social affairs, it is still an assumption that a man or woman belongs to the Church of England in the absence of definite evidence to the contrary, and it is easier for a Churchman or Churchwoman than for a Dissenter to secure social acceptance or appointment to office. With the decline of Nonconformity in recent years—and still more with the dissolution of its former close association with the Liberal Party—the difference has become much less sharp; and there are nowadays many more people in the higher ranks of society who cannot be ranked as either Churchmen or Dissenters, because they have no contact with organized religion. There are also, to complicate the position, more Roman Catholics, and Catholicism has become more powerful and more readily accepted as militant Protestantism has declined. But the Established Church has still a great weight of traditional gentility on its side; and there is still a marked tendency for those who have risen, or hope to rise, in the social scale to shed Dissenting connec-

tions and, if indifferent, to offer at least a minimum of conformity to the Church. It is a standing joke that the army
recruit who does not affirm outright any other religious
allegiance is always written down as belonging to the Church
of England.

Moreover, the social distinction between clergymen of the
·Church of England, as such, and Dissenting ministers, as
such, still persists. The former rank as 'gentlemen' *ex officio*:
the latter, though they may be individually accepted on
other grounds, do not. True, the consequences of not being
accepted as a 'gentleman' are nowadays much less far-
reaching than they used to be, because of the greatly increased numbers of well-to-do and educated persons whose
status cannot be measured by using the older categories; but
there are wide areas of society over which attempts are still
made, often very foolishly, to divide the world into 'gentlemen and ladies' and 'the rest'.

IV. THE BUSINESS AND PROFESSIONAL FACTORS

These categories—'gentlefolk' and 'common people'—
have, of course, never fitted the world of business; and they
have long ceased to fit even the highest levels of professional
work. They rest essentially on aristocratic assumptions which
presume the existence of a landed aristocracy deriving the
main part of its income from the land. They depend, too,
on an enlarged conception of the family which is closely
connected with that of a land-owning aristocracy. The
'gentleman' in the strict sense of the term is someone who is
either a landowner with tenants under him or closely enough
related to such a landowner to be entitled to claim some
share in his family prestige. The landowner's home, which
constitutes him, even if he has no hereditary title, 'Mr.
So and So of Such and Such', serves as a point of focus for a
wide circle of relatives, who define their social status in
terms of his. Wealth based on commercial or industrial enterprise has usually a much narrower circle of recognized connections, except for a few great families of hereditary

financiers or capitalists; and it has usually a much shorter line of hereditary succession. Through most of the nineteenth century, despite the rise of commercial and industrial fortunes, the gentry still maintained an attitude of theoretical exclusiveness based on lineage, and a pretension that anyone who became engaged in commerce or industry was somehow degrading himself unless he could also maintain his position in the landed hierarchy—and, even if he could, unless he was occupied at the very highest levels, as a colliery owner or banker or railway director ornamenting a board rather than participating directly in its affairs. This pretension to gentility based on the institutions of squirearchy came to correspond less and less with economic realities as industry and commerce gradually displaced land as the main source of high incomes, and as the landowners themselves came to depend on commercial and industrial investments for an increasing proportion of their revenues. But to a great extent the landed families stuck to their social pretensions even when they had come to have much smaller incomes than the leading industrialists. It follows that those who deemed themselves 'gentlefolk' by virtue of their relationship to the landowners included a high proportion of persons of quite small incomes, and that the children of these poor aristocrats had to seek for means of earning a living that they could contrive to reconcile with their social pretensions. The Church, the army and navy, and the higher branch of the legal profession did not offer nearly enough eligible openings; and they were compelled to legitimize a number of other professions as consistent with the avocation of gentleman. Medicine came to be one of the most important of these openings, and the expanding Civil Service another. The rise in social estimation of the general practitioner in medicine and of the higher clerk in the Civil Service is closely connected with this need of the 'gentle-folk' to find wider openings for paid employment. The profession of solicitor also rose steadily in social esteem; and with the rise of the 'public schools' and the revitalization of the Universities other openings were found in the higher branches of education. Ordinary school-teaching, as distinct from school-mastering in a 'public-school', remained in low esteem; and so, for a long time, did accountancy and the other rising professions directly related to business. But the place of the East India Company's service, which had been early legitimized because of the high rewards it offered, was taken by the expanding overseas branches of the Civil Service as the British Empire expanded, especially during the second half of the nineteenth century.

There was, indeed, in the growing professions a great deal of room for the children of the outer circles of the old aristocracy. But in these new fields, as well as in the higher branches of commerce, the 'gentlemen' were forced to rub shoulders with other entrants who were making their way up from lower down the social scale. The Scots, above all in medicine but also in other professions, helped to bridge the gap between 'gentlemen' and 'others', because no one quite knew how to fit them in to the English social structure; but a great number of them, coming south to find openings which Scotland did not afford, had to be fitted in somehow. The mixture of 'gentlemen' and 'not-gentlemen', according to the old definitions, in the professions did a great deal to break down the exclusiveness based on family connections, and to merge the outer groups of those connected with 'county families' into the developing upper middle class. By stages, 'upper-middle-classness' came to be more a matter of educational standards and social manners than of family connections. The comradeship of the 'old school tie'—that is, of having been to a 'public school'—gradually replaced over a wide field of professional work the 'gentlemanly' status based on ancestry, though never superseding it altogether. Moreover, those who retired from business with their fortunes made mingled more and more on equal terms with those who had never needed to work for a living. There emerged a new class of superior persons, whose pretensions were based, not on the inherited possession of unearned incomes, but on the possession of resources derived either from businesses in which they no longer took an active share, or from professional earnings, or from a mixture of the two. This upper middle class of public school products |

and of their wives is one of the most characteristic social groups of the nineteenth century, and it still holds a key position in the filling of the higher positions both in public life and the civil service and in the more esteemed professions.

Long after the higher professions had become legitimized over a wide field as open to 'gentlemen' without consequent loss of status, most kinds of capitalist business activity continued to carry some social taint. Capitalist business went through a complicated series of evolutions in the acquisition of a social status corresponding to its economic power and importance. Till well after the middle of the nineteenth century the predominant form of business enterprise was that of partnership, with joint stock structure, based on widespread ownership, prevalent only in a few exceptional fields—notably railways and commercial banking. Under the partnership system, many industrialists, especially in the textile and iron industries, made large fortunes; and some of these bought land and set about founding families in imitation of the landed aristocracy. But many more did not aspire to become 'aristocrats', and felt, indeed, a keen dislike of aristocratic pretensions and of the ascendancy of the landed interest. These created a new middle class, ranging in wealth from greatness to quite moderately comfortable circumstances; but, as long as partnership continued to be the main form of enterprise, there was a social gulf between them and those whom they employed, usually at somewhat low salaries, as hired managers and officials. The development of joint stock enterprise over a wider field, chiefly from the 1870s onwards, had a great effect in narrowing the gap between the 'employers' and the salaried employees of the larger business concerns. Where business was depersonalized by the growth of companies with large bodies of shareholders, the salaried managing director came to occupy a status equivalent to that of a considerable employer. The 'works manager' did not, as a rule, share in this social promotion: he continued to be excluded from the widened circle of 'gentility', and to some extent still is. But the managerial status rose rapidly in the final quarter of the nineteenth century and subsequently as industry came to be more affected by scientific developments and to require a higher proportion of managerial workers trained in scientific or other specialized techniques. These developments acted very unevenly in different industries: at their most considerable in the rapidly expanding steel, engineering, and chemical, and presently in the electrical industries, they did a great deal to raise the status of the managerial class; but they had relatively little influence on the textile industries until the advent of rayon, or on the greater number of the industries producing final consumers' goods. In the branches of production in which scientific discovery played the greatest part, there emerged a considerable class of qualified technicians whose most successful practitioners secured promotion into the upper levels of business leadership; and side by side with these technicians the accountants and financial experts achieved a similar rise in incomes and in social esteem. A social gap came to be recognized between these upper managerial workers and the general run of factory managers who were devoid of other qualifications than those based on practical experience. The one group began to fuse with the professional classes on a basis of equivalent technical qualification: the other ranked socially rather with the class of shopkeepers and with the lower ranges of professional work that had not acquired a recognized status of 'quality' under the new conditions. The wider opportunities for scientific and higher technological education offered through the new Universities facilitated this process; and although the lower ranges of technical education were slow in developing—much slower, for example, than in Germany—enough qualified persons were produced to staff the higher positions in the industries most dependent on scientific techniques. Little impact was made, however, on the character of managerial personnel outside these industries, partly because the 'family business', usually converted to joint stock form, held its own in most of the less scientifically based branches of production, so that the higher positions continued to be filled more by inheritance than by selection on grounds of personal qualification or capacity.

V. WORKING-CLASS ÉLITES

Élites, however, are not formed only at the higher levels of the social structure: they arise everywhere, where there is a call for leadership and administrative competence. While the new middle classes were being formed and were fusing in part with the older aristocracy based on land, the working classes were throwing up their own leaders from among those who had failed, or had never sought, to climb the economic ladder into a higher class. Two movements— Trade Unionism and Co-operation—played the predominant part in this evolution of working-class *élites* as leaders of an opposition which claimed democratic rights against both the old aristocracy and the new capitalists and their several bodies of dependants and subordinates. Of these two, Trade Unionism was much the greater social force. Co-operation, beginning as a strongly idealistic movement inspired by the vision of a new social order, and, under the influence of Robert Owen, challenging for a time the entire structure of capitalist society, quite soon settled down to operate peacefully within the environment of capitalism, as a predominantly trading movement mainly conducted by officers who had to adopt much the same methods as their private trading rivals. Trade Unionism, on the other hand, had a long fight for the very right to exist, and found itself, even when it was not challenging the capitalist system itself, continually struggling with the capitalists for a bigger share in the product of industry. The Co-operative movement had little difficulty, by appealing on the score of its value as an agency of mutual thrift, in securing from Parliament all the legal recognition it needed for its growth. It was legitimized in the 1850s almost without a struggle—for there was then no strongly organized private trading interest ready to oppose it. Trade Unionism did not win its charter of rights till the 1870s, as a sequel to the widening of the parliamentary franchise in 1867 to include a considerable proportion of the skilled workers; and even then it did not win without much struggle, or without playing off one political party that hoped to secure the working-class vote against its rival. Nor was the recognition accorded to it nearly so complete as the Co-operative movement had achieved some time before.

The Trade Unions, as the strongest and most stable upholders of the claims of the working classes, became the means of bringing into effective existence a new democratically based *élite*. This was a gradual process. Up to the middle of the nineteenth century, broadly speaking, the only stable Trade Unions were local bodies of skilled craftsmen, usually too small to be able to employ full-time officials. Most of their officials did their trade union work in their spare time, or at most as a part-time employment. Even so, there existed numerous little *élites*, chiefly among the skilled workers, composed of men who were active in their local Trade Unions and in many cases participated also in wider political movements, such as Chartism and the campaigns for factory reform. But a great change came when gradually, from the 1850s to the 1870s, the Trade Unions of the skilled craftsmen, the miners, and the textile workers began to join up into bigger units, regional or nation-wide, and to employ an increasing body of full-time officers, drawn from their own ranks, to manage their affairs and to undertake the developing business of collective bargaining with the employers which followed on the gradual concession by one employing group after another of 'recognition' of the claims of the Trade Unions to negotiate on behalf of their members concerning the basic conditions of employment. The new status won from Parliament in the 1870s was followed by a rapid extension of this form of 'recognition'; and the numbers of full-time trade union officials grew correspondingly, both because there was more to be done and because it could be done best by men who, not being employed workers, were not liable to victimization by employers for standing up for working-class claims.

Until the late 1880s, these developments were mainly limited to the more skilled sections of the working class. The labour upheaval symbolized in the great London Dock Strike of 1889 brought in a considerable contingent of less skilled workers, and therewith a further large increase in the number of full-time trade union officials. These men—

and with them a very few women—while keeping their intimate connection with the class from which they had been drawn and acting as its leaders, necessarily came to live, as administrators and organizers, a life closely akin to that of a large section of the lesser middle classes. But, continually recruited from below and dependent for their positions on the giving of satisfactory service to those who had chosen them for leadership, they did not, like workmen promoted to supervisory or managerial positions in business, become assimilated to a higher class—at any rate, not till much later, when the entire position of the Trade Unions in the social structure had been radically altered by the increased political and economic power of the organized workers, and even then only to a very limited extent. They constituted rather an *élite*, identified in sentiment with the working class and separated from the sections of the middle classes nearest to them in income-levels and in habits of living by their functional hostility to the accepted structure of classes and of class prestige. Nevertheless, there was a growing tendency for their children, as the parents became able to offer them the chance of higher education, to climb out of the working class into the ranks of the professional or managerial classes. This process has of course been greatly aided by the growth of state secondary education and by the easier access to the Universities resulting both from this growth and from the institution of scholarships financed from public funds.

Out of the Trade Unions have come a high proportion of the men who, having acquired leadership among their fellows in industrial affairs, have passed on into Labour politics. The Labour Party, in its early years, consisted largely of trade union leaders, with a seasoning of Socialists drawn mainly from the professional classes; and the Trade Unions, especially the miners, had been sending their men to the House of Commons, as allies of the Liberals, long before a separate Labour Party came into being. Nowadays, the direct part of the Trade Unions in sending their leaders to the House of Commons is relatively smaller than it used to be; for the local Labour Parties, which are mainly responsible for the choice of candidates, draw their nominees from a wide field, and there are many more middle-class Labour supporters competing for nomination with the Trade Unionists. Nevertheless, the Trade Union contingent still forms the solid core of the Labour Party in Parliament, and also on the Councils in charge of Local Government; and Trade Union activity is one of the principal ladders by which men who have left school early can climb to positions of high political influence. One reason why the Co-operative movement has been a much less important ladder is that Co-operators often prefer to choose their nominees not from their full-time officials but from the 'lay' membership of their representative agencies.

It is sometimes argued that one effect of the wider diffusion of opportunities for higher education will be to lower the quality of leadership in the Trade Unions and in other working-class bodies. As more of the active and promising young people, instead of being forced to leave school early for economic reasons, are able to carry their school educa-tion to higher levels and in many cases to reach the Univer-sity, the segregation of *élites* inevitably tends to take place earlier in life, and the working classes are left to depend for leadership more on those whose intellectual faculties develop late or, in default of enough of these, on men and women of inferior mental calibre. There is some force in this; but the tendency is at present more than offset by the better educa-tional chances offered to those who do leave school early, and it is doubtful whether the extension of high educational opportunities has yet gone far enough to weaken seriously the element of potential *élite* remaining in the working classes. I incline rather to the view that there has been hitherto so much thwarting of abilities latent in children coming from poor households that the improvements at the lower levels are likely for some time to outweigh the tendency for the working classes to be deprived of good leadership by the early promotion of promising children to a higher occupational level.

I confess that I am more worried by the great growth of alternative, largely non-political and non-economic, open-ings for the use of leisure. The workman who made himself a leader used often to go through an intense effort of study in order to fit himself to act as spokesman and thinker for his fellows. Some still do this; but the easing of economic circumstances, coming together with the immense development of purely recreational activities and the decline in seriousness of the popular press, has made it harder to increase the numbers ready to make the effort as fast as the demand for their services has been growing. Moreover, with the very advance of the Labour movement in power and prestige has gone a diminution of the evangelistic fervour which moved the pioneers. One hears frequent lamentations that the crusading spirit of the early Socialists and of the leaders of the 'New Unionism' of sixty years ago has been dying away since Socialism and Trade Unionism have become respectable and the sheer human misery which stirred the emotions of the pioneers has been both much reduced and pushed much more out of sight. But, whether or not there has been a waning of enthusiasm, the working classes still produce leaders, and throw up everywhere their own *élites* to run the endless business of collective bargaining, joint consultation in the workshops, municipal politics, national politics, and a host of other associative activities which call out, in the aggregate, an immense volume of mostly unpaid social service.

VI. THE LESSER PROFESSIONS: THE 'BLACKCOATS'

Meanwhile, there has been, as we saw earlier, a great growth of the professional and managerial classes, and of consciousness of unity among them. The major professions—for example, doctors and professional engineers—have become much more strongly organized, and more disposed to imitate at need trade union methods which they formerly despised. There has been, over the same period, an even greater growth of professional spirit and solidarity among those doing professional jobs at lower levels—from supervisory workers in industry to such groups as nurses and clerical employees. For well over a century each successive decennial Census of the population has shown the professional classes increasing much faster than the general average. This has been partly due to the recognition of new professions, which has proceeded apace; but is also a natural outcome of economic advance. Doctors and lawyers multiply with the growth of the middle classes: business, as its scale expands, throws up a host of new professions—accountants, engineers, and, later, business consultants; and both developments mean more work for architects, surveyors, bankers, and many other professional groups. Each profession brings in its train lesser professions which depend upon it, or serve as assistants to its members—apothecaries, nurses, law clerks, lesser accountants, draughtsmen, statisticians, bank managers, and many more. There is a multiplication of special qualifications for all the various grades of professional service —from university degrees, to various kinds of diploma or certificate offered by a variety of agencies, some by the organized professions themselves, and others by external examining bodies, acting sometimes under statutory powers. The consequence is that, while the higher professions are busy improving their social and economic status and in many cases endeavouring to establish, where they can, monopolies of duly qualified practitioners, a host of new groups are rising from lower down the social scale, claiming to be recognized as professional workers, and establishing in their turn standard qualifications for the right to practise their several callings. These lesser professions give rise to a whole series of secondary *élites* within the broad group of professional occupations, and help to create new forms of social and economic stratification.

Meanwhile, business, as it increases in scale and takes on the form of joint stock enterprise over a wider field, employs many more salaried managers and financial administrators at many different levels. But, unlike the professions, management has shown little or no tendency, until quite recently, to regard itself as a profession, to demand special qualifications in its own right, or to close its ranks against the unqualified. Of course, as productive technique advanced, many more managers came to require technical qualifications for their particular jobs; but, save in a few special cases, they became qualified as technicians, and not as managers. The notion of specialized training in the art or science of management as such is relatively new, and has not yet made much practical progress. Traditionally, the manager has often worked his way up from operative status through promotion first to supervisory and then to managerial appointment, picking up by the way such technical qualifications as the job has called for. This, as we saw, has been less the case in those modern industries which depend most on applied science and higher technology; but even in such industries there are a considerable proportion of managerial workers who have made their way up from the ranks. Such men, standing for the most part either on the verge of the professional class, or definitely outside it, constitute a large group in present-day society, comparable in economic position with the trade union and co-operative officials, but with an essentially different social outlook.

One effect of the rapid increase in the number of professional or semi-professional jobs and in the blackcoated occupations has been a considerable change in the relation of family to social class. An open society, which allows much scope for ascent to higher economic and social levels to individuals who possess the required qualities, necessarily tends to break up the class-solidity of the family. The individual who secures promotion to a higher position may elevate his own children to his new social group, but does not necessarily carry with him either his parents or his brothers and sisters. Admixture in the same family of members following occupations of different social prestige or carrying different social connections occurs most of all in the lower ranges of non-manual work, where the greatest numbers of new recruits are called for by the changes in occupational distribution. The increased employment of women in the professions and in clerical occupations has been a big factor in this process. Both women teachers and women clerks and typists have been drawn largely from the families of manual workers, and have made the social structure more complex than it used to be. Until quite recently, most of these growing bodies of minor professionals and 'blackcoats' showed little social coherence or capacity to throw up leaders or *élites* of their own—though the teachers were ahead of most others in this respect. Most of these groups were slow to form Trade Unions for their collective service, or even professional associations of any real strength; and when they did associate they often seemed uncertain about the purposes their associations were meant to serve. On the other hand they showed, in Great Britain, very little tendency to develop a 'fascist' outlook. That came mainly in countries which suffered from really extensive and long-continued unemployment among those who had gone through processes of higher education. In Great Britain, though 'blackcoat' unemployment did exist on a substantial scale during the inter-war period, it was never nearly severe or protracted enough to drive large numbers of the potential 'salariat' into despairing revolt or espousal of gospels of hatred for democracy. This was perhaps partly because the growth of opportunities for higher education had, right up to the 1920s, rather lagged behind than got ahead of the openings for the higher employments; but it was also, I think, because British class-divisions were, and had been for a considerable time past, less acute than those of the countries in which Fascism was able to exert a more powerful appeal.

VII. THE SOCIAL COMPOSITION OF PARLIAMENT

British society is in fact an increasingly open society, in which class mobility has been increasing considerably for the past generation. It is no doubt still less open than American society, which, from an exceedingly mobile situation, has been moving in the opposite direction. It is also less mobile than Australia, or New Zealand; but I think it is considerably more mobile than most of Western Europe. I am under no illusion that the composition of Parliament is more than one small example of this mobility, or that any assured conclusions can be drawn from a single example. It is, however, perhaps worth while to take a glance at the social composition of the modern British House of Commons and to compare it with that of certain past Houses of Commons; and the Parliament of 1950 had the advantage for this purpose of a very near balance between the two major party groups which nowadays almost monopolize the representation.

I have set out in the accompanying table a rough classification of the occupational status of the 615 Members of Parliament elected in 1950. Such a classification cannot be exact, because there are inevitably some persons who could be assigned to more than one group and also some who, being either professional politicians pure and simple or persons living on private incomes, cannot be classified at all on a basis of occupation. Despite this, the classification is good enough to give a reasonably correct impression. I have put the Labour Party M.P.s into one column, and have grouped all the rest together, as it is not worth while for the purposes of the present analysis to separate out the few Liberals or to break up the Conservatives and their allies according to their secondary differences of party label.

THE SOCIAL COMPOSITION OF THE BRITISH HOUSE OF COMMONS IN
1950

Labour Party		*Other Parties*	
Trade Union Officials (salaried)	66	Stockbrokers and Underwriters	10
Other Trade Unionists (manual workers)	31		
Political and Co-operative Officials (salaried)	16	Political and Trust Officials	10
Clerks and Insurance Workers	15	Diplomatic Service	7
Civil and Local Government Servants	6	Civil and Colonial Servants	6
University Teachers	17	University Teachers	3
Other Teachers	27		
Journalists and Authors	24	Journalists and Authors	14
Barristers (practising)	28	Barristers (practising)	42
Solicitors	12	Solicitors	11
Ministers of Religion	4	Ministers of Religion	1
Doctors and Dentists	9	Doctors	3
Accountants and Business Consultants	5	Accountants and Business Consultants	10
Other Professional Workers	9	Other Professional and Managerial Workers	10

132

Labour Party		Other Parties	
Managerial Workers	12	Surveyors and Architects	7
Employers, Merchants, and		Employers, Merchants, and	
Company Directors	13	Company Directors	85
Retail Traders and Hairdressers	5	Landowners	10
Farmers	4	Farmers	9
Housewives	4	Housewives	2
Ex-service men (regulars)	3	Ex-service Officers (regulars)	29
Unclassified	5	Unclassified	41
	315		310

The table shows, I think, that, as far as Parliament can be regarded as a meeting-place of *élites* drawn from different fields of social action, the British House of Commons of 1950 had a remarkably wide coverage. Some of the differences between the Labour Party and the other parties are interesting and significant; but I do not wish to dwell on them now. What I am stressing is that, though there is an evident tendency for the *élites* of certain groups to go into politics more than others, the British Parliament does to-day represent primarily, not a separate body of professional politicians, but rather a wide variety of social forces.

In going back into the past, I evidently cannot go into anything like the same amount of detail: nor can I make my classifications nearly so exact. As one goes back, one finds more and more Members of Parliament whom it is impossible to classify on any occupational basis. They were landowners or members of landowning families, or persons living on private incomes without any assignable occupations. Some, no doubt, were active men of business; but these have constituted a relatively small group. All I am able to do at this stage is to pick out certain very broad categories and try to see how the numbers of M.P.s assignable to each category have changed over the hundred and eighteen years since the Reform Act of 1832. I have taken only a few Parliaments, chosen for particular reasons—the first Parliament elected after the 1832 Act; the first elected after the second Reform Act (1867), which enfranchised the more skilled workers in the towns as well as a large section of the lower middle classes; the first

133

Parliament after the third Reform Act (1884), which greatly extended the franchise, especially in the country areas; the Parliament of 1900, because otherwise there would be too long an interval before the next Reform Act; the Parliament of 1918, elected after the enfranchisement of the older women; the Parliament of 1935, which seemed the most suitable after the franchise had been extended to women on the same terms as men; and the Parliament of 1950. I have avoided, where I could, Parliaments in which one party had a very big majority.

The classifications in the second table are, I know, in many respects unsatisfactory. The groups overlap—for example, where a lawyer or a military man also possessed a title—and it is very difficult to decide how many of the possessors of military titles are properly to be regarded as military men—especially just after a war. What I have done is to show separately under the later groups those who have already been included in any of the first four, and to try to count as military only persons who had been officers in time of peace.

In considering this table, it has to be kept in mind that the class of titled persons was being continually enlarged by new creations and conferments of dignities. Of all the peerages and baronetcies existing in 1939, more than one-third had been created since 1900, more than half since 1850, and more

REPRESENTATION OF CERTAIN GROUPS IN THE BRITISH HOUSE OF
COMMONS AT VARIOUS DATES

	1832	1868	1885	1900	1918	1935	1950
Titled Persons:							
(a) Lord, or Higher Title (including Irish and courtesy titles)	65	49	33	16	12	21	9
(b) Sons of Peers (Honourable)	47	47	26	34	23	19	11
(c) Baronets (Sir—hereditary)	46	41	50	57	58	40	12
Hereditary Titles—Total	158	137	109	107	93	80	32

	1832	1868	1885	1900	1918	1935	1950
(d) Knights (Sir—non-hereditary)	44	28	55	41	82	75	21
Army Officers:							
(a) included above	6	3	5	2	19	12	1
(b) not included	45	38	30	48	93	84	49
	51	41	35	50	112	96	50
Naval Officers:							
(a) included above	3	1	2	—	2	3	—
b) not included	9	3	5	1	6	11	6
	12	4	7	1	8	14	6
Air Force Officers:							
(a) included above	—	—	—	—	—	—	—
(b) not included	—	—	—	—	2	1	4
	—	—	—	—	2	1	4
Higher Lawyers (K.C., Q.C., Serjeant):							
(a) included above	1	1	3	6	6	7	3
(b) not included	4	21	31	33	17	19	17
	5	22	34	39	23	26	20
Doctors of Medicine:							
(a) included above	—	—	3	1	—	2	—
(b) not included	1	5	9	6	12	9	7
	1	5	12	7	12	11	7
University Professors:							
(a) included above	—	—	—	—	2	—	—
(b) not included	—	1	2	—	4	1	2
	—	1	2	—	6	1	2
Total individuals included	261	233	241	236	309	280	138

than two-thirds since 1800. Only one-fifth dated further back than 1750. The hereditarily titled class was being continually replenished from the ranks of country gentlemen, bankers and financiers, and, as the century advanced, from successful business men and the very highest ranks of the professions. In spite of this, its representation in the House of Commons fell almost continuously, and had its most dramatic decline between 1935 and 1950. The number of military and naval officers fluctuated considerably; but it too fell off sharply in 1950. The higher lawyers increased greatly after 1832, but declined after 1900. The other professions had few representatives until quite recently, but have now, as we saw, come to contribute a large quota to both the main party groups. The figures, let me repeat, are only very rough; but they are near enough to the truth to convey a broadly correct impression.

In Cabinets, and in the tenure of lesser ministerial offices, the element of hereditary aristocracy remained, right up to 1945, considerably greater than in the House of Commons as a whole. With a Labour Government in office after 1945, there was of course a much bigger change in this respect than in the composition of the House of Commons as a whole. By constitutional requirement, there have to be a number of Cabinet Ministers with seats in the House of Lords; and, in practice, there must be in addition enough junior Ministers to represent the Government in debate. But these two groups are drawn in fact, when a Labour Government is in office, largely from peers who have been created by the Labour Party for that very purpose—many of them retired Trade Union or Co-operative officials, with a few of the Labour 'intellectuals' drawn from the professions. Statistical comparisons are therefore of much less use, though Professor Laski, among others, has made useful analyses of the changing social composition of Cabinets and Ministries over the past century.

Within my restricted space, I cannot follow up this question. It seems better to close this part of my study with one further table, analysing the social composition of the House of Commons of 1900, broadly on the same lines as I have

136

adopted for 1950, but with a different grouping of parties, because in 1900 the Labour Party had only two M.P.s and the considerable body of Irish Nationalists occupied a rather special position. I have here grouped Liberals and Labour, including the Liberal Trade Unionists, together, and have shown the Irish Nationalists separately, and the Conservatives and their allies—Liberal Unionists and a few others —together.

OCCUPATIONAL COMPOSITION OF THE BRITISH HOUSE OF COMMONS IN 1900

	Liberal and Labour	Irish Nationalists	Other Parties	Total
Bearers of Hereditary Titles, including Courtesy Titles down to Honourable	9*	1*	60*	70*
Landowners	6	3	32	41
Army and Navy Officers	5	2	49	56
Diplomatic and Indian Services	1	—	7	8
Employers, Merchants and Company Directors	84	19†	142	245
Stockbrokers	1	1	3	5
Barristers	27	7	50	84
Solicitors	10	6	8	24
Journalists and Authors	7	13	8	28
University Teachers	6	1	7	14
Other Teachers	4	2	1	7
Doctors	2	4	3	9
Engineers and Architects	2	—	1	3
Civil Servants	2	1	3	6
Clerks	—	2	—	2
Political Organizers	—	1	—	1
Hotel Keepers	—	2	—	2
Farmers	—	7	1	8
Trade Unionists	10	3	—	13
No Occupation Known	14	9	44	67
Total (eliminating duplication)	188	83	397	668

* Including the following members also included under other categories: L. and L., 2; I.N., 1; Others, 22.
† Including retail tradesmen.

VIII. GOVERNMENT AND THE PUBLIC SERVICES

I must now attempt to bring together, in the form of a cursory survey of the social structure of the *élites* in contemporary British society, the main points that emerge from the largely historical treatment used in the preceding sections of this study. Power in this society is not concentrated at a single point, but diffused. I do not mean only that it is not exercised, as in totalitarian countries, under the centralizing control of a single party: I mean that it is widely shared in by numerous social groups, some within and some outside the political structure. Consequently there are in Great Britain a great many *élites*, each with its own sphere of action and influence, but not sharply separated—indeed, often overlapping in membership. Parliament includes representatives of a considerable number of these *élites*, and the M.P. does not normally lose touch with the *élite* from which he has come, or develop into a mere professional politician. He does not behave, however, merely as a delegate of his group, though he continues to be influenced by it. When matters specially affecting it are under discussion in Parliament, he may be expected to act to some extent as its spokesman; but on other issues, and even on issues affecting his own group when they involve wider considerations of policy, he will usually act with his party in the last resort, whatever pressures he may attempt to apply within his party to get it to accept the views of his group. In an extreme case, he may prefer his group to his party—e.g. on such a matter as state aid to Roman Catholic schools. But, when he finds party and group loyalties running counter to each other, he will look if possible for a compromise that will avoid an outright clash.

Parliament, however, as we saw, is by no means the only part of government in which *élites* are to be found. Its significance lies less in being an *élite* than in gathering together representative spokesmen of many different *élites* and in organizing them into parties which have *élites* of their own both inside and outside Parliament. In the constitution of these special *élites*, the political parties differ considerably

among themselves, though they show a certain tendency
towards assimilation. By tradition, the Conservative Party is
essentially a *parliamentary* party, consisting primarily of its
members in the two Houses, and according very wide
authority in policy-making to its leader, who is either actually
or potentially Prime Minister. The Labour Party, by contrast, is traditionally an extra-parliamentary organization,
based on a wide membership, with policy-making in the
hands of its annual delegate Conference elected by its affiliated bodies—mainly Trade Unions and Local Parties with
individual members as well as locally affiliated trade union
groups. Traditionally, the Labour Party in Parliament
carries out the policy which the party outside Parliament
lays down; whereas in the Conservative Party the extra-
parliamentary structure, based on the constituency organizations, is no more than an instrument of the party in Parliament and of its leader, and can only advise on policy, and
not prescribe or bind. In practice, however, these sharp
distinctions no longer hold. The Conservatives *have* to take
more account nowadays of the opinions of their organized
supporters; whereas the Labour Party, having risen to the
parliamentary position needed to form a Government, has to
consider the views of its representatives in Parliament, and
of their leader. All the same, it remains true that the centre of
the Conservative Party is inside Parliament, and that of the
Labour Party outside. This appears in the much higher
authority of the Labour Party's Executive Committee, which
is elected by the party Conference on a non-parliamentary
basis, as compared with the Conservative Executive. The
inner Labour *élite* consists of a mixture of M.P.s and executive
members who are not in Parliament: the Conservative *élite*
is still mainly a group of M.P.s gathered round the parliamentary leader.

The Liberal Party has now so dwindled as a parliamentary
force that its *élite* is necessarily to be found mainly outside
the House of Commons. By tradition, it stands somewhere
between Labour and the Conservatives. The Whig Party out
of which it emerged was fully as much centred in Parliament
as its Tory rival; but the reorganized Liberal Party which

emerged after the Reform Act of 1867 was almost from the first a battleground for contending forces. The National Liberal Federation, first organized under the leadership of Joseph Chamberlain in his Radical days, set out deliberately to transfer the control of high policy from the parliamentary representatives to the general body of Liberal supporters in the constituencies. This attempt met with only partial success, in face of the strong Whig tradition of parliamentary leadership. It made, however, a considerable impression, and created in the Liberal Party a situation of divided authority which continued right up to its practical disappearance as a parliamentary force.

The entire position of parliamentary parties in Great Britain is deeply influenced by the independence of Local Government. Each town and to a less extent each rural area or county throws up its own separate *élite*, concerned with the running of local community affairs, and possessing a wide discretion in the local application of policies nationally determined. Local politics are conducted nowadays, except in some of the smaller areas, largely on a basis of national party divisions; but the local party organizations are not mere subordinates of the central, and local government activities are much less dependent on national government sanction than in, say, either Germany or France. The men and women who have the highest influence in civic affairs are not necessarily the most active in national politics; nor, in practice, do most local Councils, once they have been elected, work strictly on party lines. The system of committees for the control of each main service encourages a sharing of responsibility by Councillors of rival parties; and in most areas only a minority of issues is dealt with strictly on a party basis. The *élites* connected with Local Government are an important part of the working social structure, especially in the larger towns; and they are recruited in these places from a wide range of social groups. Only in some of the smaller towns do local tradesmen dominate the Councils; and only in the more rural counties is it common to find control almost exclusively in the hands of the landowners and the bigger farmers.

National and Local Government alike have, besides their elected representatives, their salaried public servants. The higher positions in the national Civil Service used, because of the terms of the entrance examination to the superior administrative grade, to be filled almost entirely by men with excellent degrees from the older Universities, with very little chance for even the most highly qualified scientist or technician to climb up to the top rungs of the ladder. To-day, that situation has been considerably altered, though the preference for Oxford and Cambridge arts graduates has not been entirely removed. The growth of the newer universities, the improvements in public secondary education, and changes in the subjects of examination and in the values assigned to them have thrown the higher grades of the Civil Service much more widely open to scions of lower-middle-class families; and wartime changes have increased the chances for scientific and technical specialists to ascend to higher levels of promotion. Yet even to-day the Civil Service *élite*, though it is no longer so 'gentlemanly' or as classically minded as it used to be, is largely dominated by the traditional culture of 'public school' and older University, and forms a closely knit group whose members both exert a very strong influence on day-to-day administration and are quite capable of getting together in order to discredit as unworkable some innovation on which the hearts of their respective Ministers appear to be set. The Treasury officials, at the very heart of the Civil Service, exercise a very powerful influence over the disposal of appointments; and this influence tends to be conservative, not so much in a party sense as in standing out for the maintenance of the established practices of administration and against the incursion of 'outsiders' into the higher ranks of the hierarchy.

The Local Government service, on the other hand, being almost entirely independent in its recruitment and promotions of any central control, has grown up at haphazard and on a much less exclusive basis. It has taken, except for certain specialist positions in the education service, few recruits from the older Universities. and not very many from the new. A very high proportion of its members have entered it straight from school at sixteen or seventeen, and many of the occupants of the higher posts have worked their way up from this starting point, acquiring necessary qualifications for specialist work by spare-time study. Solicitors have occupied a good many of the key offices as Town Clerks, and have trained professional juniors by the old method of personal apprenticeship. For the most part, local government officers, even of the higher ranks, do not pretend to belong to the higher intelligentsia of the 'public school' and university type. They are much more like the managerial workers in business enterprise and tend to mix socially rather with this group than with the upper members of the older professions. This distinction has become a good deal less sharp than it used to be as the older professions themselves have become less socially exclusive; but, by and large, it still persists to a quite considerable extent.

The Local Government service, like the Civil Service, has its own *élites*, organized largely through various professional associations of Town Clerks, City Engineers and Surveyors, Directors of Education, and so on. It is coming, with the development of planning activities, to include a much larger element of professional specialists; and it throws off its own range of lesser professions with their own qualifying examinations and standards. Many of these professions, greater and lesser, are found both inside and outside the public service; and, where this is so, the proportion of the members in salaried public or institutional employment, as against those in fee-earning private practice, tends to increase. Professional solidarity cuts across the divisions between public employees, employees of private business, and independent consultants or practitioners; and *élites* thus intermingle. Sometimes a profession is found offering an united front to the world: sometimes its members are in conflict one with another on account of other loyalties.

Where governments do more, officials as well as elected representatives are bound to count for more in social leadership. The considerable widening in the social basis of recruitment to the Civil Service and the increased prestige of the service of Local Government have had much effect already in undermining the aristocratic and upper-middle-class foundations of British bureaucracy and thus in enabling it to respond to changes in the distribution of power at the level of the elective institutions of Central and Local Government. This is an aspect of the developments in higher education described in a previous part of this essay. But the old forces are still very strongly entrenched in certain parts of the Civil Service—notably the Foreign Office and the Diplomatic Service; and, in the Local Government service, the small proportion of recruits taken in at the highest educational levels has its consequences in a continuing weakness of leadership except in the most progressive areas.

IX. EPILOGUE

It is always difficult to compare one's own society with others. A man who has lived for a long time in a society other than that in which he grew up to manhood may be able to make a fair comparison: one who has not done this is necessarily at a disadvantage. Moreover, a man's knowledge even of his own society depends a great deal on the extent to which he has moved about and lived his life in it in diverse environments. He who knows only London—I mean, by actually living there—no more knows Great Britain than he who has lived only in Paris knows France. Of course, the same could be said of a man who has passed his whole life in a single provincial town or village. The matter, however, is one not only of geographical but also of social mobility. If I count it as part of my good fortune to have lived in the North of England as well as in the South and to have been a frequent visitor to friends and relatives in Scotland, I regard it as no less fortunate that I have been an itinerant teacher of adult working-class students as well as a university teacher, and that my Socialist connections have brought me a wide range of human contacts outside the middle-class environment in which I was brought up.

On the basis of this personal experience, as well as of my historical studies, I am disposed to say that the characteristic quality of British society is the facility with which one and the same individual can be connected with a number of different, but overlapping, social groups. Of course, this freedom is greater for the relatively well-to-do—but not necessarily for the wealthy—than for the really poor. Width of social associations costs money, but is not a necessary consequence of possessing it. American studies have shown that there is a correlation between family income and the number of formally organized associations to which the members of the family belong; and I have no doubt this holds good for Great Britain as well. The question, however, is not one simply of membership of formally constituted bodies: it is fully as much one of the diversity of unorganized social contacts. A society in which men tend to associate with the same sets of individuals for nearly all purposes may acquire a great intensity of group life, expressing itself in a strong sense of inner community among the members of each all-purpose group; whereas a society in which men group themselves differently for different purposes may be in danger of losing the coherence which comes of close all-purpose association. But the more diversified group structure has great advantages wherever there is a strong enough overriding sense of unity to hold the entire society together.

Great Britain seems to me to possess in a high degree this diversity in unity. Wherein the ultimate cause lies I am not at all prepared to say; but certainly the diversity of religious belief and its expression in many sects not very sharply marked off one from another has had a great deal to do with its development. Religious toleration, turning gradually into a recognition of something approaching equality of religious rights, has had a big influence on the growth of the whole political and social structure on a basis of diversity within the unity conferred partly by geography and partly by economic development and political unification.

Inevitably, a diversified and non-exclusive group life, which renders possible for the individual attachment simultaneously to a number of overlapping groups, affects the quality of leadership and the character of social *élites*. A non-overlapping structure of groups involves the emergence of *élites* which represent and mould the behaviour of each group as a whole, and of all the individuals contained in it. There may indeed be in such a structure rival bodies of leaders struggling for mastery within a single group; but each will be seeking mastery over the group in all the aspects of its members' lives. As against this, where groups are more fluid and diverse, and their memberships overlap considerably, *élites* will tend to emerge more on a functional than on a general basis, and the individual will tend to respond to different leadership in different spheres of feeling, thought, and action. Conflicts will be to some extent transferred from the groups to the individuals within whose minds they will appear as conflicts of personal loyalties. In the absence of a strong general unity binding all the groups and individuals together in a common society, the consequences of such a structure will appear in personal tensions and neuroses; but, given a sufficient basis of general community feeling, the consequence will be a great enrichment of personal life and liberty. A society organized in this manner will not have either a single *élite* presiding over all its affairs, or a number of rival *élites*, each at the head of a distinct faction of its people: it will have instead numerous *élites*, whose authority over it will be not general but functional and particular. No doubt, to a considerable extent, each *élite* will have its own following, composed of persons to whom the function that it exercises makes a strong appeal; but even such followers will be feeling also the normally less powerful pulls of other loyalties, and at the same time each *élite* will be exercising some pull on the attitudes of many who do not accord it the first place among their loyalties. It is all, of course, a matter of degree; but, broadly speaking, each *élite* will have to content itself with a less absolute and exclusive leadership, and the real government of the society will be in the hands of social forces which act, not separately, but through a process of interpenetration and intermingling at every level of the formation of opinion and of decision upon courses of action. Continuous compromise, rather than revolution, will be characteristic of such a society, which will be eternally repugnant to the apostles of 'all or nothing', whatever their 'all' may be. There will be much less room than in other societies for what Max Weber called the 'charismatic' leader; but there will be also much more real self-government, and much more chance for the common man and woman to find out the ways of life that suit them—always provided that there is enough underlying unity to hold so diversely articulated a society together.

VI

British Class Structure in 1951

CLASS, from whatever point of view it is regarded, is a very complicated concept. It eludes definition, unless it is somehow qualified, by such words as 'economic', or 'social', or 'income'; and even when the qualification has been made the elusiveness remains, to the extent that no two enumerators, working independently, could be expected to arrive at even approximate agreement about the number of individuals, or households, in a given society to be assigned to the various classes, even if they had agreed in advance on the names of the class-groups they were setting out to quantify—which might itself prove to be no easy matter. There are, indeed, so many different approaches to the whole problem that the very names to be given to the various classes are a matter of unending dispute. The Marxist thinks primarily in terms of the great contrast between 'capitalists' and 'proletarians', or, when he is dealing with the past, of other ruling classes, such as the 'feudal'; and he fits in other groups which he finds it necessary to recognize by giving them qualifying adjectives—for example, *petit bourgeois* or *lumpenproletariat*. The Marxist is at any rate attempting to base his classification on a clearly formulated principle, by defining classes in terms of their relation to the 'powers of production'. But when he turns from his general theory to any attempt at statistical measurement the difficulties begin; for a great many individuals and a great many families cannot be assigned with certainty to any one class in terms of this defining principle. He may argue that this does not matter, because the classes he speaks of exist whether they can be precisely enumerated or not; and it can be argued that a lack of precision is of minor importance if we can feel assured that the main groups have been rightly marked out. But there remains the question whether the method of definition in terms of each class's relation to the 'powers of production' is the best, or the only valuable, way of approaching the problem. It certainly does not yield, when it is used for measuring the number of persons belonging to each class, any result which coincides either with income differences or with differences of prestige or esteem in any particular society to which it is applied. Nor is it at all easy to relate the Marxist categories with any approach to precision to the information made available in such sources as the Population Census or other returns dealing with 'man-power' in a particular country. This, it may be said, is because the statisticians responsible for collecting the data have not asked the right questions. But what are the right questions?

In dealing with the assessment of class there are at least three different ways of setting out. Class can be regarded, as the Marxists among many others regard it, as an objective phenomenon, so that, subject to marginal exceptions, each individual can be put into a definite class-pocket in terms of one or more defined characteristics of his situation in society. The chosen criterion may be his relation to the 'process of production' or the size of his income or possibly the age at which he left school or some other objective characteristic— or perhaps a combination of several such characteristics. If, however, more than one criterion is used, subjectivity is bound to enter in, for it becomes necessary, when different criteria lead to different conclusions, to decide to which the primary importance is to be allowed. The second way of approach is the directly subjective—that of asking each person to say to what class he holds himself to belong, and accepting the answers as valid. One trouble about this method is that the answers may be much affected by the terms in which the questions are put—as in the well-known instances in which the substitution of 'lower' for 'working' as the name given to the class to be distinguished from 'upper' and 'middle' has notoriously influenced the replies. The third method—much the hardest to apply in practice—

is that of estimating a person's class by finding out the views of his friends and neighbours; for this involves very elaborate questioning, is open to the same difficulty in respect of the names given by the investigators to the various classes, and in addition gives rise to awkward problems when friends and neighbours differ in their assessments. In theory, I suppose, the investigator could start without making any suggestions about class-names or categories; but if he did he would be confronted with a set of answers which would be too discordant to be added up and would be rendered largely meaningless because the answerers would have widely different notions about the meaning to be given to a question about class unaccompanied by any elucidation of the sense in which the word was being used.

These difficulties are so well known that there is no need to discuss them in any detail in the present study. My purpose here is to take the recently published data for the British Census of 1951, and to see what light can be derived from them concerning the present class structure of British society. The preliminary reports in question, it should be pointed out, are based, not on the full examination of the Census schedules, but on a random sample of one per cent of the total. They may therefore not yield precisely correct results, especially in relation to some of the smaller groups; but they are not likely to be so much out as to invalidate any important conclusions that can be derived from them. Their serious shortcoming, from the standpoint of their use in considering class structure, is first that they rest on a list of occupations which is in some respects inadequate because it groups too many categories together; and secondly that the assignment to a particular class is made, not for each individual, but for each occupational group as a whole, so that, for example, all 'farmers' constitute a single group irrespective of the importance of their holdings, and 'managers' are picked out as a separate category only for some occupations, whereas in others they are mixed up with 'operatives' and in others are included in a residuary category of 'managers' in general, without assignment to a particular line of business.

The Census authorities, in dealing with the problem of class, work mainly on the basis of an arbitrary division of the occupied population into five 'social classes' placed one below another in a descending order. The top class is composed mainly of the higher professions and of such persons as can be grouped together under the heading of higher 'managers' or directors of business enterprise. It includes all ministers of religion, officers in the armed forces, lawyers, professional scientists, authors, journalists, and medical doctors; but it excludes all teachers and all artists, as both these groups are relegated to Class II because they consist mainly of less well paid professionals. In other words, the whole of each name-group is assigned to the same class, and the possibility of breaking up a group depends on it having been given a distinct name for the purpose of enumeration in the Census. Thus, higher Civil Servants are distinguished from middle Civil Servants, and put in Class I, because there are definite grade names for the two categories, whereas there are no such formal names for the higher and lower administrative and managerial groups in the majority of occupations. In the present sample survey all railway officials are put in Class II, whereas some road transport officials are assigned to Class I; and so on.

Class II in the Census classification is made up largely of shopkeepers and farmers, to whom are added the secondary professions, such as teaching and nursing, and a substantial number of managerial groups not deemed worthy of inclusion in Class I.

With Class III, by far the largest, the Census enters on much more debatable ground. Into this class are put, as far as possible, all foremen and supervisory workers, clerks, shop assistants, typists, and blackcoated workers, together with all manual workers who are regarded as belonging to predominantly skilled trades. The conception of skill is here extended not only to jobs which are learnt by some form of apprenticeship or formal learnership, but also to a great many trades in which there is no clear dividing line between craftsmen and semi-skilled workers. The effect is to create an enormous middle group, which in my analysis I have done my best to break up by separating off, where I could, the supervisory and non-manual workers on the one hand and the manual operatives on the other, forming two class-groups standing, not one above the other, but broadly at the same social class level. These I have called IIIA and IIIB.

Class IV is meant to consist of semi-skilled workers, standing between the 'skilled', in the broad sense given to the term in the Census, and the unskilled workers, who are in some cases labourers permanently attached to a particular industry or occupation and in others a floating group of more or less casual workers. This unskilled category makes up Class V.

It needs to be emphasized that this method of classification by occupational groups cannot be treated as equivalent to an attempt to classify each individual. It is meant only to give a rough idea of the proportions in the population as a whole and in the main types of occupation who belong to each 'social class', on the assumption that the entire occupied population can be reasonably sorted out into five classes in a definite order of precedence. For some purposes the Census authorities themselves use a slightly elaborated classification into 'socio-economic groups'. This separates the agricultural section from the rest and treats the armed forces as a separate group. For some other purposes the Census uses a quite different classification, by 'industrial status', into employers, managers (divided into three grades), high-grade operatives belonging to Social Classes I and II, other operatives, and workers on own account, omitting the unemployed. But unfortunately this 'industrial status' classification is not given in full detail and cannot be fully worked out from the available data for more than a limited number of types of employment. In what follows, I shall make some use of both these alternative classifications, where they are applicable; but their uses are limited in view of the paucity of data.

The Census tables deal for the most part with numbers of individual persons; but they deal also with households, and an attempt has been made in them to assign each household to a 'Social Class', by taking the occupation, past or present, of the male householder as the sole criterion. It seems simplest to begin this study by looking at the results of this attempt, which are presented in Table I in two forms. The first column shows the classification into the five Social Classes, according to the class-grading of the householder's occupation: the second gives the rather more elaborate grading into what the Census calls 'Socio-economic Groups'.

It will be seen that the simpler grading into five classes puts about half the total number of households into the middle group and that the slightly refined classification into Socio-economic Groups puts more than half into the five middle categories. Thus, on either basis, we start with about half the households in the middle, with roughly 22 per cent above them and between 29 and 27 per cent below. The grouping is of course very rough. All farmers, shopkeepers, and small employers are assigned to Class II and to Groups (1), (4) and (5), though a good many of each of these categories will obviously be earning less, and will have a lower social status, than a good many supervisory or skilled manual workers or clerical employees. The two classifications therefore both tend to over-estimate the size of the category or categories standing between the top grade, which is identical for both, and the middle Class or Groups. If half the farmers and shopkeepers and small employers were moved down into the middle grade, the effect would be, in terms of Socio-economic Groups, to leave only 14 per cent in the next higher group of grades, and to increase the middle grades to 55·7—which probably gives a more realistic picture. If, instead of a half, one-third of those in the three categories were moved down, the next higher grades would include 16·3 per cent, and the middle grades would be raised to 53·4 per cent.

In the table I have divided the middle Socio-economic Groups (6 to 10)—into two sub-groups, roughly non-manual and manual, treating those engaged in Personal Services as manual, and shop assistants as non-manual workers. This gives 12·2 per cent in the non-manual group and 38·7 per cent in the skilled manual grade. If half the shopkeepers and small employers are added to the middle non-manual group,

TABLE I

HEADS OF HOUSEHOLDS IN GREAT BRITAIN, 1951

Classified by Social Class and Socio-economic Group. Excluding Households whose head is retired or unoccupied

(figures in thousands)

	Social Class			Socio-economic Group		
	Number	*Per cent*		*Number*	*Per cent*	*Per cent*
I	411·4	3·3	(3) Higher Administrative, Professional, and Managerial workers, including large employers	411·4	3·3	3·3
II	2,263·1	18·3	(1) Farmers	323·9	2·7	
			(4) Intermediate Administrative, Professional and Managerial workers, including Teachers	1,377·5	11·2	
			(5) Shopkeepers and small employers	605·6	4·9	18·8
III	6,111·0	49·5	(6) Clerical workers	623·5	5·1	
			(7) Shop Assistants	388·1	3·1	
			(9) Foremen and Supervisors	490·3	4·0	12·2
			(8) Personal Services	511·7	4·1	
			(10) Skilled workers	4,271·2	34·6	38·7
IV	2,028·3	16·5	(11) Semi-skilled workers	1,387·5	11·2	
			(2) Agricultural labourers	513·7	4·2	15·4
V	1,523·4	12·4	(12) Unskilled workers	1,390·8	11·3	
			(13) Armed Forces (other ranks)	42·0	0·3	11·6
Totals	12,337·2	100		12,337·2	100	100

Households unclassified because their heads were unoccupied or retired numbered 2,144·3 thousand or 14·8 per cent of the total. If they are included in the total as a separate group the percentages for the five Classes in Column 1 become—Class I, 2·8, Class II, 15·7, Class III, 42·2, Class IV, 14·0 and Class V, 10·5.

L

this becomes 14·7 per cent; and a similar addition of half the farmers to the middle manual group raises it to roughly 40 per cent. If these transfers are limited to one-third, the figures for the middle groups become roughly Non-manual, 13·8, and Manual 39·6 per cent. In rough approximations, we shall not go far wrong if we rank 3·5 per cent of all the households, classified according to the occupations of their heads, in the top grade, 15 to 16 per cent in the second grade, about 14 per cent in the non-manual middle grade, about 40 per cent in the manual middle grade, and 15·5 and 11·5 per cent respectively in the two lowest grades. Say 19 per cent above, and 27 per cent below the middle grades, which together account for roughly 54 per cent.

This grading, it should be borne in mind, is in terms of households and not of individuals, and excludes all households whose heads are unoccupied or retired. It is impossible, by Census methods, to classify the unoccupied. The retired can be classified by their former occupations as stated in the Census form; but former occupations may be a very misleading guide to present status; and on this ground they have been omitted from the table. The effect on the 'Social Class' percentages of including them as a separate category is shown in the footnote under the table; but these figures are not significant for the purposes of the present study.

Let us now turn from households to individuals—that is to say, to individuals who are either 'occupied' or 'retired' according to the Census classification, which counts the non-employed as 'occupied' when they describe themselves as available for work, or have retired from 'gainful occupations'. In Table II, however, and in the other tables which follow, the non-employed and the retired are shown separately from those actually at work at the time of the Census, and no attempt is made to assign either of these groups a particular status. Table II, though it makes use of the 'Social Class' groupings in certain respects, is drawn up in terms, not of Classes in a descending order but of groupings delimited by the form which their employment takes. It shows a total of 24,424,300 persons over fifteen—17,205,560 males and 7,218,800 females—or, deducting the retired and

TABLE II

STATUS AGGREGATES, GREAT BRITAIN, 1951

Total occupied and retired population aged fifteen and over

(in thousands)

	Males	%	Females	%	Total	%
Employers	405·9	2·6	54·0	0·8	459·9	2·1
Managers, General, and Directors	167·0	1·1	18·4	0·3	185·4	0·8
Managers, Branch or Primary Departments	368·9	2·4	81·3	1·2	450·2	2·1
Managers, Office or Subsidiary Departments	101·2	0·6	11·4	0·2	112·6	0·5
Operatives, Class I and II	1,299·7	8·5	761·5	11·2	2,061·2	9·3
Operatives, Others	12,106·0	79·0	5,633·4	82·9	17,739·4	80·0
Working on own account	887·4	5·8	237·2	3·5	1,124·6	5·1
Total Working	15,336·1	100	6,797·2	100	22,133·3	100
Out of work	326·1		119·1		445·2	
Retired	1,543·3		302·5		1,845·8	
Total	17,205·5		7,218·8		24,424·3	

the out of work, 22,133,300 persons, made up of 15,336,100 males and 6,797,200 females.

According to the figures given in Table II, rather more than 2 per cent of all occupied persons, excluding the retired and the out of work, are 'employers' of one sort or another, and 0·8 per cent in addition are in high directing or managing positions. Of course, many of these 'employers' are very small, and it must have been difficult to draw a line between some of them and the 'workers on own account', who number rather more than 5 per cent of the total. The 'Own Account' group, on its side, must include a number of professional workers who work on their own, without employing labour beyond a clerk or secretary. Classification by 'status', in this sense, cannot be expected to coincide, even approximately, with the division into 'Social Classes', which is based much more, in the Census figures, on considerations of income and social prestige than on the relation of the persons classified to the 'processes of production'. It is significant that, whereas Table I showed more than 7·5 per cent of all heads of households as belonging to the farming, shop-keeping, and small employer groups, Table II shows as employers only about one in fifty of the occupied population, as against more than one in twenty working on 'own account'. The 'employer' and 'own account' groups together account for only 7·2 per cent of all occupied persons. The discrepancy is, no doubt, partly accounted for by the relatively small number of women in the 'employer' groups. If we take males only, 'employers' and workers 'on own account' together make up 8·4 per cent of the total.

Indeed, Table II brings out very clearly the differences in occupational status between men and women. The 'Operatives' group, excluding operatives assigned to Social Classes I and II, accounts for nearly 83 per cent of all occupied women, as against 79 per cent of occupied males. Women, in proportion to their numbers, hold a greatly inferior position to that of men throughout the employing and managerial categories—2·5 per cent of the total of occupied persons as against 6·7 per cent for the males. They come into their own only in the group of 'operatives' assigned to Social Classes I and II, in which they make a higher percentage than the men, no doubt chiefly because of the higher proportion of women in professional and other non-manual occupations. In the 'Own Account' group they fall back to their position of proportional inferiority—3·5 per cent of all occupied women as against 5·8 per cent of all occupied males. Women also hold, in proportion to their numbers, many fewer managerial positions than men at all levels, the inferiority being least at the 'Primary Department' level, at which it is 1·2 per cent of the female total as against the 2·4 per cent of the men.

For some purpose it is best to use the figures for occupied

males only. Table III shows the particulars for the 17,205,500 occupied and retired males whom the Census authorities have attempted to apportion to the five 'Social Classes'. In this case, the unemployed as well as the retired are included in the estimates, at the cost of some additional uncertainty on account of the difficulty of determining the 'Class' to which such persons ought to be assigned. On this basis we again get 3·3 per cent in Class I—the same figure as we got for heads of households; but this is probably not significant, as the retired and unemployed have presumably been assigned to this Class on a proportional basis.

TABLE III

SOCIAL CLASS DISTRIBUTION IN GREAT BRITAIN, 1951

Occupied or Retired Males only

(thousands)

	Under 25	25–45	45–60	Over 60	Total	% of total
Class I	61·3	252·0	144·7	109·8	567·8	3·3
Class II	157·9	1,039·4	782·1	562·8	2,542·2	14·8
Class III	1,771·2	3,888·4	2,060·6	1,315·0	9,035·2	52·5
Class IV	464·5	1,105·5	730·3	525·7	2,826·0	16·4
Class V	310·2	774·9	623·7	525·5	2,234·3	13·0
	2,765·1	7,060·2	4,341·4	3,038·8	17,205·5	100

Percentages of each Age Group in each Social Class

	Under 25	25–45	45–60	Over 60
Class I	2·2	3·5	3·3	3·6
Class II	5·7	14·7	18·0	18·5
Class III	64·1	55·1	47·5	43·3
Class IV	16·8	15·7	16·8	17·3
Class V	11.2	11·0	14·4	17·3
	100	100	100	100

Percentages of each Social Class in each Age Group

	Under 25	25–45	45–60	Over 60	
Class I	10·8	44·4	25·5	19·3	100
Class II	6·2	40·9	30·6	22·2	100
Class III	19·6	43·1	22·8	14·5	100
Class IV	16·5	39·1	25·8	18·6	100
Class V	13·9	34·7	27·9	23·5	100

In Class II we now get only 14·8 per cent, as compared with 18·3 per cent of the households; but this difference is not surprising, as the figure for all occupied workers will obviously include a considerable proportion of young males who are not yet householders and have not yet reached the highest positions they will occupy at some time during their working lives. This classification of all occupied males shows 52·5 in Class III, as against 49·5 per cent of the householders. For Class IV the proportions are practically the same; and for Class V the difference—13 per cent as against 12·4 per cent for householders—is not significant when we bear in mind the low proportion of those in the armed forces who are heads of households. The significant difference, then, is in Class II, and must be accounted for mainly by the inclusion of a larger number of young people.

When we turn in Table III from the total number in each Social Class to their age-distribution,[1] we find, as we should expect, that the proportion of persons in Class III is highest in the youngest age group—under twenty-five years of age—whereas all the other classes reach their maximum in the group of sixty years and over. A certain number of those who begin in Class III will subsequently rise into higher classes, and a certain number will fall into a lower class as they pass middle age. As retired persons are presumably classified in relation to their previous occupations, Social Class III will undoubtedly include a number of persons of very low private income—for example, among pensioners; and to this extent the figures must be used with caution. A worker who, before he retires, falls into a lower occupational group, through illness or disability, may very well give, after retirement, the occupation to which he belonged in his prime.

10·8 per cent of the persons in Class I, as against only 6·2 per cent of those in Class II, are in the youngest age-group. This is presumably because Class II is made up to a greater extent than Class I of persons who are promoted into

---

[1] This has been worked out for male persons only, because women have, on the average, a much shorter occupied life and are much more difficult to assign to 'social class' categories resting on occupation.

it after reaching the age of twenty-five. The difference has greatly narrowed in the next age-group, and has been reversed in the third and fourth. For the same reason, the age-group forty-five to sixty has the highest proportion of Class II's total membership as against other Classes.

We have been dealing so far with highly general categories, without any attempt to break them up into separate industrial or occupational groups. It is indeed impossible to do this, except for a limited number of groups; for neither the occupational nor the industrial tables given in the Census sample volumes furnish the requisite information. In Table IV I have brought together, as a preliminary presentation, what I have been able to get out of these volumes about the class structure of a number of branches of economic and social activity in respect of managerial and professional structure down to the supervisory level. This Table is still based on the five-class conception of 'Social Classes' but relate sonly to those members of Classes I, II, and III who can be assigned to a particular branch and can be regarded as exercising managerial, administrative, professional, or supervisory functions. It thus leaves out most of Class III (e.g. clerical workers and shop assistants, as well as skilled manual workers) and also those members of Classes I, II, and III who, though they hold managerial or supervisory positions, are not shown in the Census tables separately from the main body of Class III. It will be seen that the information is particularly deficient about manufacturing industries, for most of which it is impossible to find the required information in the Census volumes. Even where figures of a sort can be found, their limitations are all too evident; but they are at least better than nothing at all.

In the first column of Table IV the leading professional groups classified by the Census in Social Class I are assigned to the broad groups of occupations. As far as industry is concerned, this classification shows a high concentration of higher professional workers in the metal, chemical, and building and contracting groups. This is the result of assigning the various bodies of professional engineers and of scientists connected with chemistry and metallurgy to these

TABLE IV

AN ANALYSIS OF THE PROFESSIONAL, MANAGERIAL,

Industry	Professional Class I		Directors and Managers Class I		Managers and Administrators Class II	
Mines and Quarries	Mining Engineers	4·0			Mine Managers	12·8
Metal, Vehicle, and Electrical Trades	Metallurgists Mechanical Engineers Ship Designers Electrical Engineers	4·4 27·5 2·1 20·6			Managers, etc.	101·4
Chemical Trades	Chemical Engineers Chemists (not Pharmacists)	5·5 24·7			Managers, etc.	17·3
Textile and Clothing Trades					Managers, etc.	50·5
Food, Drink, and Tobacco Trades						
Building, Woodworking, and Contracting Trades	Civil Engineers Architects, etc.	27·7 19·1			Managers, etc.	50·1
Transport Trades			Omnibus and Tram Shipping	2·4 6·2	Car and coach Garage Air Transport Wharfingers and Stevedores Others	4·9 19·7 0·6 9·4 18·4
Land and Agriculture	Surveyors	37·6			Farmers and Managers Bailiffs, etc. Estate Managers and Agents	316·8 18·3 2·4
Commerce and Distribution					Wholesalers Brokers, Agents, Factors Sales, etc., Managers Retailers	114·2 52·8 33·8 623·9

TABLE IV

Professionals, Officials, and Staffs *Class II*		*Managerial and Executive* *Class III*		*Supervisors* *Class III*	
				Mine Deputies, etc.	47·5
Draughtsmen	126·8			Foremen, etc.	121·8
				Foremen, etc.	12·4
				Foremen (Textiles) Overlookers, etc.	29·3
				Foremen (Boots and Leather)	7·1
				Foremen, etc. (Clothing)	11·8
				Foremen, etc.	18·5
Clerks of Works	9·7	Builders (unspecified)	56·0	Foremen and Gangers	60·0
				Foremen (Painting)	10·9
				Foremen (Upholstery, etc.)	1·8
Railway Officials	21·3	Haulage Managers and Contractors	20·0		
Road Transport Inspectors	16·7	Foremen (not Rail)	14·6		
Dock and Harbour Officials	5·3				
Air Officers and Pilots	12·5				
		Market Gardeners, etc.	58·0	Market Garden Foremen	3·8
Commercial Travellers	140·4				

TABLE IV—(*continued*)

Industry	Professional Class I		Directors and Managers Class I		Managers and Administrators Class II	
General Business and Finance	Solicitors	22·8	Company Directors	3·0	Office and Dept. Managers	60·8
	Barristers	3·3	Company Officials	30·5	Misc. Industrial Managers	64·9
	Economists and Statisticians	3·5	Bankers and Bank Managers	18·6	Moneylenders, etc.	1·9
	Accountants (qualified)	37·3	Insurance Managers	27·9	Auctioneers and Valuers	23·5
			Stockbrokers and Jobbers	4·5	Managers (unspecified)	0·9
					Others in Finance	4·4
Entertainment and Catering					Hotel keepers	27·5
					Boarding House keepers	48·9
					Innkeepers	72·1
					Restaurant keepers	86·9
					Theatre and Cinema Managers	7·9
					Other Entertainment Managers	3·4
					Producers and Stage Managers	4·6
Public Services	Officers (Armed Forces)	46·2	High Civil Svts.	12·1		
Health Services	Doctors and Radiologists	44·1			Veterinary Surgeons	4·6
	Dentists	13·6			Trained Nurses and Midwives	171·9
					Physiotherapists	10·3
					Radiographers	5·1
					Pharmacists	13·8
					Opticians	6·8
					Other Medical Auxiliaries	27·8
Education and Science	Biologists	2·1			Social Workers	22·6
	Physicists	3·8			Teachers	356·7
	Other Scientists not given elsewhere	11·4			Librarians	15·2
					Matrons and Stewards (not Hospital)	25·2
Other Occupations	Ministers of Religion	48·1			Religious Workers	9·0
	Authors and Journalists	28·8			Society Officials	5·5
					Artists	17·4
					Misc. Professional Workers	23·7

162

TABLE IV—*(continued)*

Professionals, Officials, and Staffs Class II		Managerial and Executive Class III		Supervisors Class III	
Industrial Designers	6·2	Insurance Brokers and Agents	71·6	Foremen (unspecified)	13·2
Financial Clerks, etc.	489·9	Bookmakers	13·8		
Executive Civil Servants	68·9	Other Civil Servants (not Clerks)	11·8		
Local Government Officials	29·0	Other Local Govt. Officers (not Clerks)	3·8		
Police Officials	6·0				
		Chiropodists	5·9		
		Laboratory Workers	71·2		

groups and of the inclusion of a large number of architects in the building and contracting group. Most industries have no similar groups of professional or scientific workers who can be assigned to them, though of course the majority of them give some employment to high-grade professional and scientific workers, There is, however, a real distinction between the industries in which the high development of scientific techniques requires a considerable body of well qualified applied scientists and technicians and those in which such techniques still play a relatively minor part. The engineering and metal-working industries and the electrical and chemical industries are the principal groups to which this great dependence on scientists and technicians extends. The building and civil engineering industries are rather differently placed, in that, whereas civil engineering depends greatly on professional technicians, in building the technical element is relatively small, and the high proportion of professionals is due mainly to the inclusion of architects and quantity surveyors.

Outside industry there are large concentrations of professional workers belonging to Social Class I in the Public Services (including commissioned officers in the Navy, Army, and Air Force), in the Health Services (doctors and dentists), in the land and agriculture group (surveyors), and in the general and miscellaneous groups. The main elements in the General Business and Finance group are lawyers (barristers and solicitors) and qualified accountants, and in the 'Other Occupations' group ministers of religion, and authors and journalists. The Census assigns all ministers of religion and all authors and journalists to Social Class I, whereas it puts all artists in Social Class II, and all actors in Social Class III, presumably because it has been found impracticable to break up these groups into sufficiently distinguishable subgroups assignable to different Social Classes. Similarly, all teachers are put in Social Class II, though obviously, on any individual assessment, a number of them would be assigned to Social Class I and others to Class III. Here again we encounter the necessary limitations of an assignment based on occupational categories rather than on the income or the prestige attached to a particular kind of job within each broad occupational group.

In Table V I have summarized for convenience, under a number of main heads, the data given in Table IV. The summary brings out very clearly the inadequacy of the data for any estimate of the numbers in the higher managerial and administrative groups in manufacturing industries. For the most part industrial administration and higher management are lumped in with managers and administrators of the second grade. This applies to railways and mines as well as to manufactures: indeed the only groups in which the higher grades can be distinguished at all are the Civil Service (Administrative Class) and some branches of transport and finance. The main group of higher administrative and managerial workers appears under the heading 'General Business and Finance', and has as its largest elements company officials, insurance managers, and bankers and bank managers. All railway officials, down to stationmasters at small stations and 'agents' of lower rank, are lumped together in a single category.

Tables IV and V have similar limitations in respect of the lower professions and of the lower grades of management and administration. The largest group by far which I have assigned to the lesser professional category consists of financial clerks, bookkeepers, and cashiers, whom the Census separates from the general category of clerks. This very large group, which numbers nearly half a million, is obviously in fact exceedingly heterogeneous. It includes all the less qualified workers in accountancy, including cost accountancy, together with a very wide range of bookkeepers, cashiers, etc., attached to a host of types of enterprise and varying greatly in income and social status. There is, however, no effective way of breaking it up on the basis of the occupational tables. The next largest category of clearly professional workers in Social Class II consists of draughtsmen, whom it has been necessary to assign wholly to the Metal and Electrical group, though obviously a number of draughtsmen are employed in other types of enterprise. Rather more numerous than the draughtsmen are the commercial travellers, whom I have included in the Table with some hesitation, as assignable to the secondary grade of either professional or managerial workers.

Supervisory workers of course exist in every type of enter-

TABLE V

A SUMMARY ANALYSIS OF PROFESSIONAL, MANAGERIAL, AND
SUPERVISORY OCCUPATIONAL GROUPS

	Class I		Class II		Class III	
	Professional	*Managerial*	*Professional*	*Managerial*	*Professional and Managerial*	*Supervisory*
Mines and Quarries	4·0	—	—	12·8	—	47·5
Metal, Vehicle, and Electrical Trades	54·6	—	126·8	101·4	—	121·8
Chemical, Rubber, and Plastics Trades, and Chemical Science	30·2	—	—	17·3	—	17·6
Textile and Clothing Trades	—	—	—	50·5	—	36·4
Paper and Printing Trades	—	—	—	—	—	15·5
Food, Drink, and Tobacco Trades	—	—	—	—	—	18·5
Building and Contracting	46·8	—	—	59·8	56·0	72·7
Transport Trades	—	8·6	12·5	96·3	20·0	—
Land and Agriculture	37·6	—	—	337·5	58·0	3·8
Commerce and Distribution	—	—	—	824·7	140·4	—
General Business and Finance	66·9	84·5	496·1	156·4	85·4	13·2
Entertainment and Catering	—	—	—	251·3	—	—
Public Services	46·2	12·1	—	103·9	15·6	—
Health Services	57·7	—	238·3	—	—	5·9
Education and Science (not listed elsewhere)	17·3	—	419·7	—	71·2	—
Other occupations	76·9	—	55·6	—	—	9·6
Totals	438·2	105·2	1,349·0	2,011·9	446·6	362·5

prise; but it is not possible to mark them off in all cases from other grades. The persons identified in Table V as belonging to such groups number 362,500; but this figure is exclusive of the numbers in the various branches of transport, commerce, and distribution, in which they are lumped in either with managerial employees belonging to Social Class II or with other 'staff' workers assigned to Social Class III. Similarly, no distinct supervisory group can be identified from the Census data for the Public Services or for Entertainment and Catering. In all, the number of persons in the supervisory groups—foremen and overlookers and their equivalent in 'service' occupations—must be well over half a million; but no precise figure can be given.

Among the groups for which figures do exist, by far the largest is to be found in the wide category of metal, engineering, vehicle, and electrical trades, and the next largest in building and contracting. In both these groups the traditional structure is that of bodies of skilled craftsmen, aided by labourers or less skilled workers and by apprentices, working under the supervision of foremen who have been drawn from the ranks of the craftsmen. But whereas this structure survives to a considerable extent in the building industry (much less in civil engineering) it has been largely overgrown in the metal and engineering trades (but not in shipbuilding) by a more complex structure in which the larger part of the actual operation of machines used for repetitive work has passed into the hands of semi-skilled machine operatives, and many of the skilled workers have become setters-up of machines operated by others. This system involves, in addition to the skilled setters-up and maintenance men, a large contingent of workshop supervisors who occupy a status somewhere in between the lower grades of management and the main body of skilled craftsmen, but are by no means always better paid than the latter. A somewhat similar structure exists in other mass-producing branches of production; whereas in the printing trades there has been only a much smaller corresponding growth of an intermediate group of semi-skilled workers. In the mining industry the foreman is replaced by the deputy, who performs an analogous rôle. In the textile trades, the overlooker differs in certain respects from the foreman, and in some branches is more nearly analogous to the setter-up. All the groups included under the heading of supervisory workers are, however, fairly similar in status, in that they are mainly recruited from among the skilled craftsmen, or in some cases from among skilled women workers, and stand in a somewhat difficult position between the management and the workers they are responsible for supervising at the level of the workplace or department in which they are employed.

In Tables IV and V I have been using what the Census authorities call an 'occupational' as distinct from an 'industrial' classification. The difference between the two is simple in principle, though not always easy to apply. A bricklayer who is employed in a steelworks comes into the 'occupational tables' under the building trades, but into the 'industrial tables' as a worker attached to the steel industry. A railway clerk is 'occupationally' a clerk but 'industrially' a railway worker; and so on. Let us now turn to the 'industrial' tables and see what further light they throw on the class structure of the British occupied population.

In the 'industrial' tables, as we saw, the basis of sub-classification is no longer mainly 'Social Class' but 'Industrial Status'. Instead of the five 'Social Classes' we get a different break-up into employers, great and small together; directors and general managers; managers of branches and main departments; managers of offices and subsidiary departments; persons classified as 'operatives' but assigned to Social Class I or to Social Class II; and workers on own account. Thus, the concept of Social Class is invoked in these tables only for the purposes of breaking the wide category of 'operatives' into two sub-categories—which are quite different from the two sub-categories into which I broke up Class III in analysing the occupational tables. The sub-category of operatives shown in Table VI consists entirely of persons who are not managerial, but are regarded as belonging to one of the two highest Social Classes. They are, in effect, mainly lesser professional workers and technicians employed in the various industries and services to which they are assigned.

In Table VI I have not attempted to give figures for every industry or service, and in a number of cases, I have had to use very broad groupings, partly because the Census sample tables give fewer details about women than about men. At the head of Table VI, however, I have put the general figures for all the industrial groups listed in the Census tables. The purpose of Table VI is to show how the make-up of the total personnel varies, in terms of the proportions in the different 'status' categories, from industry to industry. I wish it were possible to show for each industry the proportion of supervisory as well as of managerial and professional workers; but the Census 'industrial' tables furnish no information on this point, and it is not possible, with any approach to even approximate correctness, to use the occupational figures for this purpose.

It appears from Table VI that, over the whole field of 'industries' (including services) in the Census sense of the term, one occupied person out of every five is either an employer or a manager of sorts, or a professional or technical worker in Social Classes I or II, or a worker on 'own account' —that is, self-employed. The other four are 'operatives', including supervisory workers, belonging to Social Classes III, IV, and V. Of course, many of the workers 'on own account', and some of the smaller employers, also belong to these three Classes; but these persons cannot be separated from other workers 'on own account' or from employers who are higher up in the social scale. The classification here is in the main functional, and not in terms of income or even of social standing. It has, however, seemed worth while to separate the group of workers 'on own account' from all the other listed categories and to show in the third column from the last the percentage of all these other groups to the total numbers in employment. It should be observed that Table VI, unlike some of the earlier tables, excludes the unemployed as well as the retired. It deals only with persons who were actually in employment at the date of the Census.

Over 'industry' as a whole there is a preponderance of men over women, proportionally as well as absolutely, in all the superior categories. This is not at all surprising; for even

TABLE VI

STATUS IN RELATION TO INDUSTRY

(percentage of totals actually employed—'out of work' excluded)

	Sex	Employers	Directors and General Managers	Branch and Department Managers	Office, Subsidiary Department Managers	'Operatives' in Social Classes I and II	Total of Preceding Columns	Workers on Own Account	All Others
All Industrial	M	2·6	1·1	2·4	0·7	8·5	15·3	5·8	78·9
Groups	F	0·8	0·3	1·2	0·2	11·2	13·6	3·5	82·9
	T	2·1	0·8	2·0	0·5	9·3	14·8	5·1	80·1
Professional	M	5·6	0·4	1·1	0·4	51·6	59·1	8·4	32·5
Services	F	0·4	0·1	0·2	0·1	44·8	45·6	2·8	51·6
	T	2·5	0·2	0·5	0·2	47·6	51·1	5·1	43·8
Mining and Quarrying	T	0·1	0·1	0·4	0·2	1·9	2·7	—	97·3
Coal Mining	M	—	—	0·2	0·1	1·6	2·0	—	98·0
Chemical	T	0·2	1·1	1·8	1·3	8·4	12·7	0·1	87·2
Metal Manufacturing	T	0·1	0·4	1·0	0·7	5·3	7·5	0·1	92·4
Engineering, Shipbuilding, and Electrical	T	0·2	0·8	1·1	1·0	7·7	10·8	1·6	87·6
Engineering	M	0·3	1·2	1·9	1·1	2·8	7·2	1·0	91·8
Electrical	M	0·3	0·9	1·5	1·9	10·6	15·1	0·3	84·6
Vehicles (inc. Garages)	T	1·1	0·7	1·2	0·8	5·5	9·3	2·4	88·3
Textiles	T	0·3	0·7	1·3	0·6	2·5	5·4	0·1	94·5
Cotton	M	0·2	1·0	2·1	0·7	3·9	7·9	—	92·1
Clothing and Leather	T	1·3	1·2	1·2	0·4	1·2	5·4	3·5	91·1
Food, Drink, and Tobacco	T	1·6	1·1	2·4	0·9	4·2	10·2	3·0	86·8
Paper and Printing	T	0·6	1·5	1·9	0·7	7·5	12·2	0·8	87·0
Building and Contracting	T	3·8	1·2	1·4	0·6	3·4	10·4	5·5	84·1
Gas, Electricity, and Water Supply	T	—	0·1	0·6	0·3	9·8	10·8	—	89·2
Transport	T	0·7	0·5	1·1	0·2	5·6	8·1	2·3	89·6
Distribution	T	4·7	2·2	6·2	0·7	7·3	21·0	9·9	69·1
Insurance and Finance	T	1·1	0·9	5·2	0·3	32·2	39·7	1·4	58·9
Catering	T	4·1	0·6	5·8	0·6	5·4	16·5	12·9	70·6
Entertainment and Sport	T	2·0	0·8	3·3	0·8	5·3	12·3	9·4	78·3
Agriculture and Fishing	T	10·6	0·2	0·8	—	3·7	15·2	20·8	54·0

apart from the traditional superiority accorded to males, many women retire from gainful employment on marriage, and the proportion of occupied women to men is lowest in the higher age-groups, which naturally include a high percentage of persons promoted to the higher grades. It is rather surprising that the over-all difference between the sexes is not greater than it appears to be. If workers 'on own account' are excluded, the average proportion of males in the higher categories is 15·3 per cent, as against 13·6 per cent for women. The smallness of this difference is partly accounted for by the relatively large numbers of women employed in non-manual callings, which have a high proportion of higher-grade to lower-grade workers. I have not thought it worth while to work out the separate proportions for men and women for the various industries, except the professional group, which has by far the largest percentage of higher grade persons. In this group 59·1 per cent of the males and 44·5 per cent of the females are assigned by the Census to the higher categories; but the proportions of workers 'on own account' are much further apart—8·4 per cent for males and only 2·8 per cent for females.

For the sexes taken together, the industrial group which shows the lowest proportion of higher-grade workers is Coalmining, with only 20 per cent. The miners are a highly paid group; but as the Census assigns all those who are counted as skilled manual workers to Social Class III, including deputies, and as the mining industry employs relatively few professional workers and technicians, the high average income level is not reflected in the 'status' classification. Of the remaining industrial groups included in Table VI, the two which show relatively fewest in the higher grades are Textiles and Clothing (including Leather), each with 5·4 per cent; but the Clothing group has naturally many more 'own account' workers than Textiles, which are constituted almost entirely of factory trades. Metal Manufacture comes next with 7·5 per cent, followed by Transport with 8·1 per cent, by Vehicles (including garages) with 9·3, by Food, Drink, and Tobacco with 10·2 per cent, by Building and Contracting with 10·4 per cent, and by the Engineering, Shipbuilding, and Electrical trades group and the Public Utilities group, each with 10·8 per cent.

At the other end of the scale, after but a long way behind the Professional Services group, comes Insurance and Finance, with 39·7 per cent of the total personnel assigned to the higher grades. Then comes Distribution, with 21 per cent, followed by Catering, with 16·5 per cent, and Agriculture and Fishing, with 15·2 per cent. This leaves in the middle positions Chemicals, with 12·7 per cent, Entertainment and Sport, with 12·3 per cent, and Paper and Printing, with 12·2 per cent. I have also shown a separate figure for men only in the Electrical industries—15·1 per cent—because this diverges rather sharply from the general percentage for the wider group in which they are included in the main figures. For the rest of the Engineering trades the corresponding figure for men only is 7·2 per cent.

Thus in manual industries, to the extent to which the Census attributions of 'status' can be accepted as correct, Agriculture shows the highest proportion of those occupied as belonging to the higher grades, and Mining (especially Coal Mining) the lowest. If we leave out Mining and Agriculture the range of difference narrows to that between the Chemical industries, with 12·7 per cent, and the Textile and Clothing industries with 5·4 per cent. All these figures leave out workers on 'own account', who are relatively most numerous in Agriculture and Fishing (20·8 per cent), with the Catering industries (12·9 per cent) second, and Distribution (9·9 per cent) third. Apart from Agriculture, the highest proportion of 'own account' workers in any mainly manual industry is in Building and Contracting (5·5 per cent), followed by the Clothing group, with 3·5 per cent.

I do not pretend that these figures are very satisfactory; but I think they are better than nothing. It is, of course, obvious that workers on 'own account' will be fewest in industries which are mainly carried on in large establishments, and relatively most numerous where there are many small firms. But there is rather more to it than that. Certain types of service, such as repair work in building, dressmaking, and boot-repairing, lend themselves readily to the one-man business, as well as to the small-scale business using hired labour; and so do certain services—small shopkeeping, some forms of catering and domestic work, and some forms of professional service, in addition to small-holding agriculture using unpaid family labour.

In Table VII, which is the complement to Table V, I have set out, as far as the Census figures allow, the distribution of persons in the various occupational groups among Social Classes III, IV, and V. This Table unfortunately has to be compiled on an 'occupational' rather than an 'industrial' basis, as the 'industrial' tables of the Census do not include any grouping by Social Classes. Nevertheless, it throws some light on the relative sizes of the supervisory, other non-manual, and skilled, semi-skilled, and unskilled manual working force in different types of employment, though the grouping of all clerks and all typists in single occupational categories makes it much less useful than it would be if these large groups could be broken up. It will be seen that the first few groups in the Table have no Class IV or Class V personnel assigned to them. This is because the less skilled workers who are attached to services of these kinds are of unspecialized or not separately classified types, such as office-cleaners and porters. In addition, in most of these cases, supervisory workers are not shown separately; and of course the numerous clerks and typists do not appear under the first four headings, but are included in the 'General Business' category. Thus, the Class III figures are made up, for the Professional group, of minor professional workers; for the Public Services Civil group, of officials other than clerical workers—largely technicians; and for the Post Office, mainly of telephonists, sorters, and telegraphists; while in the Armed Forces group the column is blank, because the Census does not distinguish non-commissioned officers from private soldiers, sailors, or airmen.

The 'General Business' group is made up, for Class III, mainly of clerks, secretaries, typists, and insurance agents. The Class IV constituents are mainly hall-porters, caretakers, and window-cleaners, and those in Class V mainly office cleaners and charwomen, messengers, and attendants

TABLE VII

DISTRIBUTION OF SOCIAL CLASSES III, IV, AND V BY OCCUPATIONAL GROUPS

	Class IIIA		Class IIIB Skilled Manual Workers	Class III Total	Class IV Semi-Skilled	Class V Unskilled	Classes IV & V Total
	Super-visory	Others					
Professional Services	—	71·2	—	71·2	—	—	—
Public Services (Armed)	—	—	523·0	523·0	—	—	—
Public Services (Civil)	15·6	126·8	—	142·4	—	—	—
Post Office	—	210·2	—	210·2	—	—	—
General Business Occupations (including all Clerks and Typists)	—	1,913·9	—	1,913·9	127·0	301·4	428·4
Commerce and Distribution	—	1,170·4	105·3	1,275·7	241·1	112·0	353·1
Health Services	—	74·1	5·1	79·2	48·1	—	48·1
Catering Services	—	112·4	159·5	271·9	378·3	206·2	584·5
Personal Services	—	25·9	5·5	31·4	479·6	—	479·6
Laundries and Cleaners	—	—	—	—	140·8	—	140·8
Entertainment and Sport	—	77·8	18·3	96·1	2·2	—	2·2
Transport							
Railway	—	—	149·7	149·7	124·2	74·6	198·8
Road	16·7	20·0	594·6	631·3	186·7	—	186·7
Water, Docks, and Harbours	—	—	61·0	61·0	38·9	84·4	123·3
Air	—	—	6·5	6·5	—	—	—
Unclassified	14·6	—	—	14·6	—	43·2	43·2
Total	31·3	20·0	811·8	863·1	349·8	202·2	552·0
Mining							
Coal Mining	44·2	—	221·3	265·5	369·9	—	369·9
Other Mining and Quarrying	3·3	—	6·9	10·2	38·6	—	38·6
Total	47·5	—	228·2	275·7	408·5	—	408·5

	Class IIIA		Class IIIB Skilled Manual Workers	Class III Total	Class IV Semi-Skilled	Class V Unskilled	Classes IV & V Total
	Supervisory	Others					
Metal							
Metal Manuf.	5·2	—	56·9	62·1	—	3·4	3·4
Foundries	7·4	5·3	88·4	98·5	61·7	—	61·7
Forgemen, Smiths Annealers, etc.	—	—	78·2	80·8	4·3	—	4·3
Engineering, etc.	37·2	7·9	396·6	441·7	108·1	—	108·1
Vehicles	—	—	187·1	187·1	—	—	—
Shipbuilding	—	—	78·7	78·7	—	—	—
Sheet Metal, Coppersmithing	23·7	—	87·4	87·4	—	—	—
Electrical	—	25·5	378·0	427·2	12·7	—	12·7
Other Metal Trades	1·7	3·0	196·1	200·8	142·5	—	142·5
Metal Trades (unclassified)	59·2	79·6	—	138·8	—	403·2	503·2
Total	134·4	111·3	1,547·4	1,793·1	329·3	506·6	835·9
Chemicals, Plastics, and Rubber	16·4	—	84·5	100·9	72·1	62·0	134·1
Glass, Pottery, Bricks, etc.	8·1	—	90·2	98·3	38·3	64·7	103·0
Paper and Printing	13·4	—	230·9	244·3	28·3	—	28·3
Textiles	29·3	—	451·6	480·9	164·0	101·1	205·1
Clothing	11·8	—	292·8	304·6	252·9	—	252·9
Leather, Boots	7·1	—	183·4	190·5	—	—	—
Total	18·9	—	476·2	495·1	252·9	—	252·9
Food, Drink, and Tobacco	18·5	—	153·2	171·7	56·3	—	56·3
Building and Contracting	70·9	60·0	417·6	548·5	24·4	462·8	487·2
Woodworking	23·0	—	324·5	347·5	14·9	—	14·9
Total	93·9	60·0	742·1	896·0	39·3	462·8	502·1
Public Utilities	16·0	6·7	17·0	39·7	29·4	26·2	55·6
Agriculture and Fishing	3·8	58·0	113·0	174·8	694·5	3·3	697·8
Other Occupations	15·2	—	314·5	329·7	310·8	555·0	865·8

of various types. In the Commerce and Distribution group, Class IIIA is made up mainly of shop assistants, roundsmen, and commercial travellers, and Class IIIB of skilled warehouse workers. Class IV consists of packers, bottlers, and similar types, and Class V of unskilled warehouse labourers. In this group it is again impossible to distinguish the supervisory workers, some of whom will have appeared as 'managers' under Class II in Table V, while others are lumped in with the shop assistants and other groups under Class III.

Again, in the Health Services group, supervisory workers cannot be separated out. Class IIIA consists mainly of sick nurses—other than the fully qualified, who appeared in Table V and were assigned to Class II. The few persons in Class IIIB are funeral workers, who seemed to fit in least awkwardly under this heading. Class IV is made up mainly of hospital attendants.

In the Catering group, Class IIIA consists of waiters and waitresses, and Class IIIB of chefs and cooks. Class IV consists of barmen, barmaids, and restaurant hands, and Class V of kitchen hands. The assigning of all waiters and waitresses, chefs and cooks to Class III, and of all barmen and barmaids to Class IV is an obvious instance of the inaccurate estimates that are bound to result from using broad occupations, rather than distinctions within them, as the basis for the determination of social class. Similar difficulties arise in the Personal Services group, in which Class IIIA is composed of children's nurses and Class IIIB of chimney-sweeps, all types of domestic servants, except nurses, being lumped together in Class IV. The next group, Laundries, cannot be sub-divided at all. Finally, in this part of the Table, the Entertainment and Sport group ranks all actors and musicians together in Class III, together with professional games-players, bookmakers, and a number of lesser categories. Class IIIB is made up of cinema operators, jockeys and racecourse workers, and Class IV of stage-hands not classified elsewhere.

In none of these groups are the classifications very enlightening. Nor is the position much better when we come to the Transport groups. In the case of Railways, all officials have been put together in a single category under Class II, which must include many supervisory workers who would be better assigned to Class III. Moreover, railway clerks are not separated from other clerks, and do not appear under the Railway heading: so that we are left with only a division of manual workers into three categories—engine drivers, signalmen, guards, and some others in Class III, firemen, running shed workers, and ticket-collectors in Class IV, and porters in Class V. The figures for Road Transport are rather better; for here the supervisory workers can be separated out from the haulage contractors in Class IIIA. Lorry, bus, and tram drivers are in Class IIIB, and conductors, mates, and (horse) carters in Class IV. In the Water Transport group, which includes dock, harbour, and canal undertakings as well as shipping, the supervisory grades cannot be shown separately; but most of the supervisory workers entered under 'Transport (unclassified)' must in fact belong here.

In the Coal Mining group, the Census authorities have taken the doubtful line of assigning only hewers and getters and underground enginemen to Class III and of relegating all other colliery manual workers to Class IV. Actually, I think a substantial proportion of the latter should be grouped with the getters in Class III; but I cannot say how many. Here the supervisors (deputies, etc.) can be counted separately; but all the other officials have been assigned to Class II, whereas some of them should certainly be in Class III. The skilled craftsmen, other than face-workers, are not included in the figures, except the enginemen underground. The rest are counted under other occupational headings with the crafts to which they belong.

The Metal group, which is the largest of all, can fortunately be broken up for a number of purposes, though not for all. The figures for Metal Manufacture—chiefly Iron and Steel—are misleading, because the fairly large body of labourers cannot be separated from those in the other metal-working occupations. The same applies to the Shipbuilding trades, and indeed to every constituent of the Metal group. But, in most of the sub-groups, it is possible to make a distinction between the skilled craftsmen and the semi-skilled workers, as well as in part to separate the supervisory workers from the rest, though only with a very large unassignable residue. If we take the Metal group as a whole, we get a clear picture of a field of employment dominated by skilled manual workers. The Chemical group, on the other hand, shows a preponderance of less skilled workers.

In the Glass and Pottery group, skilled and less skilled workers are nearly balanced. In Paper and Printing, the skilled hold an overwhelming preponderance. In the Textile group the skilled manual workers outnumber the less skilled by well over two to one. In the Clothing group, the difference is relatively small, unless the Leather and Boots group is included—in which case it becomes two to one on the side of the skilled workers. In the Food, Drink, and Tobacco group the skilled preponderate by three to one.

In the large Building and Contracting group the skilled and the less skilled are not very far apart in total numbers; but in fact the skilled predominate in Building and the less skilled in Public Contracting—largely road work. If the carpenters and joiners from the Woodworking group are thrown in, the predominance of skilled workers in the Building sub-group is increased.

In the Public Utility group—gas, electricity, and water supply—the less skilled outnumber the skilled. Finally in Agriculture (the inclusion of Fishing makes only a negligible difference), after all farmers have been put in Class II, only market gardeners and a few minor categories are left in Class III, the main body of agricultural workers being assigned as a whole to Class IV, which also includes the whole of the 29,300 fishermen.

Opposite, for convenience, are the totals, for a few groups, of those assigned respectively to Social Class III and to Classes IV and V combined, expressed as percentages of the totals in the three Classes.

This broad classification gives the Paper and Printing group a very long lead over all others, with Commerce and Distribution second, the Food Trades third, Textiles fourth, and Metals only fifth. Mining is a very long way behind, because the number of skilled mineworkers has been underestimated. Agriculture comes lowest; but we must remember

TABLE VIII

PROPORTIONS OF WORKERS IN CERTAIN OCCUPATIONAL GROUPS IN
SOCIAL CLASSES III, IV, AND V

	Class III	Classes IV & V
Transport	61	39
Mining and Quarrying	40	60
Metals	68	32
Chemicals	43	57
Paper and Printing	90	10
Textiles	70	30
Clothing and Leather	66	34
Food, Drink, and Tobacco	75	25
Glass, Pottery, and Bricks	49	51
Building, Contracting, and Woodworking	64	36
Public Utility Services	42	58
Agriculture	20	80
Commerce and Distribution	78	22
Catering	32	68

that all farmers are left out and all agricultural wage-workers counted as semi-skilled. Catering is next lowest, and then come the Public Utility and Chemical groups. Clothing, Building and Contracting, and Transport are well in the middle.

How do these positions compare with what we know about (a) earnings and (b) the proportions in which male and female workers are found in the various groups? No exact comparison is possible, because figures of average earnings are compiled on an industrial rather than an occupational basis, and a distinction between men's and women's earnings can be made only between broad industrial categories. For earnings I use the latest figures at the time of writing instead of going back to 1951; but I think this makes little difference.

The comparative Table—Table IX—brings out some startling differences. The Social Class differentiations of the Census appears to have little relation either to the differences between men's and women's occupations or to the differences of average wage-incomes in the various industries to which the occupational groups are mainly attached.

TABLE IX

EARNINGS (APRIL 1953) AND SOCIAL CLASSES (1951)

	INDUSTRIAL:				OCCUPATIONAL:	
	Weekly Earnings Men over 21	Weekly Earnings Women over 18	Weekly Earnings All workers, including Juveniles	Percentage of Operatives in Social Classes I & II	Percentage of Classes III–V in Class III	Classes IV & V
Men's Industries:						
Coal Mining	246/1	—	234/1	1·6	40	60
Dock Labour	205/5	—	—	—		
Building and Contracting	185/10	(88/5)	176/4	3·4	64	36
Other Mining and Quarrying	179/4	(99/4)	174/–	—		
Public Utilities	171/9	(96/4)	165/9	9·8	42	58
Agriculture	133/2	(88/4)	—	3·7	20	80
Industries in which men outnumber women by:						
10 to 1 Metal Manufacture	205/5	101/9	191/11	5·3	68	32
Vehicles	204/8	115/3	184/3	5·5		
9 to 1 Misc. Transport	170/8	129/1	164/2	—	61	39
5 to 1 Engineering, Electrical, etc.	196/4	107/8	171/10	7·7		
Woodworking	179/7	102/8	154/4			
Public Service	146/10	90/3	165/9	—		
4 to 1 Chemicals	186/1	100/9	163/1	8·4	43	57
Glass, Pottery, Bricks, etc.	189/11	93/7	163/7	—	49	51
3 to 1 Paper and Printing	206/5	103/3	161/2	7·5	90	10
2 to 1 Jewellery and Instruments	192/2	104/11	153/5	—		
Misc. Manufacturing	188/9	97/–	149/3	—		
Leather	173/3	94/2	134/9	—		
Food, Drink, and Tobacco	167/1	94/2	133/5	4·2	75	25
Approximately Equal:						
Textiles	177/9	102/4	128/8	2·5	70	30
Industries in which women outnumber men by:						
2 to 1 Clothing	172/6	98/7	110/4	1·2	66	34
5 to 1 Misc. Metal Trades	192/8	97/10	156/–	—		
All Manufactures	191/11	101/–	156/–	—		
All above, except Coal Mines, Docks, and Agriculture	185/11	100/3	157/7	—		

TABLE X

BROAD COMPARISON OF EARNINGS AND SOCIAL CLASS AS DEFINED
IN THE CENSUS

	Percentage of Workers in Class III. (Total of Classes III–V = 100)		Place in Order of Earnings in Table IX		
			Men's	Women's	Total (including Juveniles)
Printing and Paper	90	Printing and Paper	2	5	17
Food, Drink, and Tobacco	75	Food, Drink, and Tobacco	20	15	18
Textiles	70	Textiles	15	7	19
Metal Trades	68	Metal Manufacture	4	8	3
		Vehicle Trades	5	2	4
		Engineering and Shipbuilding	6	3	7
		Misc. Metal Trades	7	12	12
		Instrument and Jewellery Trades	8	4	14
Clothing Trades	66	Clothing Trades	17	11	20
		Leather Trades	16	16	16
Building and Contracting	64	Building and Contracting	12	18	5
		Woodworking	13	6	13
Transport	61	Misc. Transport (excluding Railways and B.R.S.)	19	1	9
		Docks	3	—	2
Glass, Pottery, and Bricks	49	Glass, Pottery, and Bricks	9	17	11
Chemicals	43	Chemicals	11	9	10
Mining	40	Coal Mining	1	—	1
		Other Mining and Quarrying	14	10	6
Other Manufacturing Trades	—		10	13	15
Public Utilities	—		18	14	8
Agriculture	—		21	19	21

Table X, in which I have put together the data from
Tables VIII and IX in order to make a rough comparison
between earnings and Census estimates of Social Class,

brings out the almost entire absence of any correspondence between the two sets of figures, whether men's and women's wage earnings are taken separately or together. It has of course to be borne in mind that the figures of Social Class are 'occupational' and those of earnings largely 'industrial', so that the comparison is not at all exact. But this cannot account for the width of the discrepancies, for the two classifications—by occupation and industry—are not different enough to lead to so wide a difference in the results. The latter must be accounted for mainly by the character of the Census differentiation between skilled, less skilled, and unskilled workers. Take two extreme cases, the Food group and Mining. The Food and Drink trades are very near the bottom in respect of average earnings for both men and women; but they are second only to the Printing and Paper group in respect of the proportion of their workers whom the Census treats as 'skilled'. Mining, on the other hand, is at the bottom of the scale in respect of the proportion of skilled workers, but, in its predominant section, Coal Mining, right at the top in respect of earnings. These results are plainly absurd. They are extreme instances of the misleading consequences of the Census method of assessing skill. What seems to have happened is that in occupational categories in which a clearly defined group or groups of *highly* skilled workers exist, and have been assigned to Social Class III, other workers of *less* skill but often of some skill, have been pushed down into Class IV, whereas in categories in which the *highly* skilled group is less clearly marked off, the whole of the groups that can claim *some* skill have been pushed up into Class III.

In some occupational groups the distinction between skilled and less skilled workers can still be drawn with some approach to reality. This is the case chiefly in occupations in which some form of regular apprenticeship is still the main, though not necessarily the only, avenue to employment on skilled work. Thus, in the printing trades, compositors still manage to maintain their insistence on apprenticeship over most of the firms in the industry and have been able to transfer their monopoly from hand to machine setting by getting control of linotype and monotype machines. The skilled pressmen have not been quite so successful, and have had to admit the claims of limited groups of outsiders; but, the outsiders once absorbed, they have largely re-established their position. The bookbinders, on the other hand, faced with the growth of machine-binding, have had to give up a good deal of ground to women workers paid at much lower rates. But, as far as I can see, the Census figures group all these categories of workers in Class III, despite the very considerable differences.

In the huge category of metal workers are included many different groups. In the shipyard trades there is a fairly clear line between the fully skilled, the semi-skilled, and the labourers; but even these last are certainly not less skilled than many groups which the Census assigns to Class III. In engineering proper, apprenticeship is still important as a road of entry to a number of fully skilled trades, which the Census assigns to Class III; but because it is easy to draw a line between these trades and the great mass of machine-operators, the latter are pushed down into Class IV, though many of them are quite as skilful (and earn more money) as many of the workers in other occupations who are classified as skilled. On the other hand, in the miscellaneous metal trades I think a good many workers who are no more than semi-skilled have been classified as skilled because of the difficulty of drawing any clear line. Sometimes, however, this difficulty works the opposite way. In the coal mines, as we saw, the classification of all workers except hewers and enginemen as less than skilled yields an absurd result. The situation arises because it is difficult to draw any clear line except for the categories which have been assigned to Class III.

The plain truth is that in nearly all trades in which mass-production by means of machines operated by single operatives (or sometimes by small squads or teams) becomes the prevalent mode of production, there arise large groups of workers who are semi-skilled, or whose skill is restricted to the operation of a particular type of machine. Where these workers work in conjunction with large bodies of more highly skilled workers—mostly the inheritors of older skills acquired by apprenticeship or its equivalent—they tend to be classified as semi-skilled. Where, on the other hand, there are relatively few fully skilled workers needed, the few there are will be in many cases classified not under the same *occupational* group as the less skilled, but together with other skilled workers in the occupational group to which their types of skill are predominantly attached—e.g. as engineering craftsmen—even if they are working in a mine or a chemical or textile factory. In such cases, the less skilled workers will tend to be pushed up by the classifiers into the skilled category, which would otherwise be left empty in relation to the occupational group in question.

This amounts to saying that the realistic information that can be derived from the Census classification is very limited as far as the distinctions between Class III and Class IV are concerned. Nor is the situation any better in respect of the distinctions between Class IV and Class V. These indeed hardly appear to rest on any principle at all.

What does emerge positively from the whole discussion of the Census figures is the very great complexity of the economic class structure in Great Britain to-day. I can only end by stating my own broad conclusions, with no pretence of being able to give them any better statistical foundation than the quicksands I have been treading in this study. Out of every hundred occupied persons, my guess is that one is either a substantial employer or a high-level business administrator; two or three are managers at lower levels, and another two small employers, including small farmers and shopkeepers. Nine or ten are professional workers, ranging from the higher professions to such lower groups as school-teachers and trained nurses; but I cannot venture to break them up into definite grades. Two or three are supervisors of various kinds—principally foremen and overlookers. Five, at widely different income levels, are working 'on their own account'; and eight or nine are clerks or typists. These groups together include at least 30 per cent and perhaps as much as one-third of the total occupied population. The remaining two-thirds or more include four or five shop assistants or other non-manual workers; and the remainder, 60 per cent at least, is made up roughly in equal proportions of four grades of manual workers—fully skilled, fairly skilled, semi-skilled, and unskilled. This is of course only a very rough approximation; and it ignores the complicating factor of juvenile workers and also the differences between men and women.

There are of course a number of other sources from which I could have drawn, for particular occupations, figures throwing some further light on status and degree of skill. But it would have been impossible to bring these further data within the scope of this study without making it far too long; and I could not in any event have used them for arriving at any *general* conclusions relating to the entire occupied population. I have therefore limited the present study to the data based on the 1951 Census, partly in order to make plain its limitations, but also in the hope of tempting other students of class structure into the field, either by inducing them to discover how much better or worse the statistics of other countries are than those of Great Britain, or by leading them to correct my very provisional conclusions by using other sources of information.

This study has left in the background certain important theoretical questions which arise in connection with any attempt to relate the concepts of occupation and Social Class. In some cases the description of a man's occupation carries with it a clear statement of his position in the class structure—for example, agricultural labourer, railway porter, or engine-driver, mule-spinner, compositor, dock labourer, shop assistant, bank clerk, university professor, chartered accountant, mine manager, postman, rivetter, bishop, police magistrate, admiral, dustman, midwife. Even within these occupational groups there are differences of status, as well as of income; but in using these words, we do at least give a broad categorization of class as well as of occupation. Many occupational terms, however, fail to carry any clear indication of class. This is the case not only where they are not specific enough—for example, manager or labourer or clerk,

N   185

without any further indication—but also where the same word is habitually used in different senses or where an occupation ranges over a number of Social Classes but cannot be satisfactorily broken up to indicate the differences in terms of any qualifying occupational description. Baker or butcher or tailor may mean either a shopkeeper or a journeyman employed at a wage in manual labour; engineer may mean either a professional belonging to one of the great engineering Institutes—Civil, Mechanical, etc.—or a skilled metal-working mechanic. The other type of difficulty—that of an occupation whose members may belong to widely different Social Classes—can be illustrated by many examples. The station-master of a big railway junction and the station-master of a small country station cannot be assigned to the same Social Class: nor can all shopkeepers (or all grocers, or drapers, or tobacconists), or all farmers, or all journalists, or all artists, or all teachers. Brokers, agents and works managers are other instances of widely varying occupations which it is difficult to break up into social class groups.

The theoretical interest of this problem arises chiefly in relation to the Marxist theory of classes, which insists that class depends on relation to the means of production. Marx used this principle, first, to categorize the opposed classes of *bourgeois*, or capitalists, and proletarians, and secondly to distinguish from both what he called the *petite bourgeoisie*. Both *bourgeois* and proletariat were related, in Marx's characterization, to the development of modern economic techniques —mechanization and large-scale production; whereas the *petite bourgeoisie* and the peasants were regarded by him as essentially related to obsolescent forms of economic structure. Marx took little account in his theory of the growing body of salary-earning technicians and administrators who, at the lower levels of these groups, were coming to constitute a new and quite different *petite bourgeoisie* interposed between the capitalists and the proletariat. These he regarded as hirelings of the capitalists, identified with their class-interests. Yet they clearly earned their livings in a different way, in the form of salaries which had more in common with wages than with profits. Nor did Marx take much account of the growing

186

diffusion of shareholding interest in joint stock enterprise, though this made partners of the active capitalists not only many passive livers upon unearned incomes but also many active managerial and professional workers whose returns on investments only supplemented their principal sources of income.

Critics of Marxism have often argued, on the strength of these and other gaps or defects in the Marxian theory, that the entire attempt to link class and occupational categories together is mistaken. Some of them have put forward theories of class as an essentially social, or 'prestige', category, having little or no connection either with occupation or with the relation of occupational groups to the means of production. This, however, is to lean over much too far in the opposite direction. It is undoubtedly possible to assign to definite positions in terms of class status the vast majority of those who belong to a large number of occupational groups, though not to all; and there is no good reason for refusing to do this because it cannot be done for every group. It is no doubt true that even within such groups as dock labourers or mule-spinners or chartered accountants or doctors of medicine there are substantial differences of class status, related in part to differences of income and in part to the prestige of particular types of job. But that does not prevent the great majority of persons in each of these groups from being assignable, with sufficient precision, to a single class.

The notion that such assignment is illegitimate naturally arises most easily in societies characterized by a high degree of social and economic mobility, such as the United States. In such societies in a pre-eminent degree, the family is apt to be a very complex institution from the standpoint of class, even if it is regarded as limited to parents, children, and immediate 'in-laws'. The children, where avenues to higher education are widely open, may enter occupations which remove them from the class-group of their parents, or they may marry out of their parents' class. As soon as the family is regarded in a larger sense, as including the kin, much greater diversities evidently appear. The occupation of the head of the household, even if it indicates his personal class, may be a quite inadequate guide to the class status of the family. But the less mobile a society is, the more nearly will parental and family class tend to coincide.

To some extent, the limitations of the conclusions that can be drawn from the data considered in this study are due to defects in the collection of the information on which the data are founded or in the analysis of it by the Census authorities. It would be possible, by framing more exact questions and by more thorough analysis, to improve the data. But it would not be possible, however well the Census authorities did their job, for them to present a clear account of the social class structure of the population as a whole. How, for example, could they break up the farmers? By the size of the holdings? This would yield most misleading results as between both different districts (according to the nature of the land) and different types of farming. By size of income? This is not the sort of question that can be properly asked in a Population Census filled in by householders for everyone dwelling under their roof. Similar difficulties apply in the case of shopkeepers, of many professional men and women, and of many kinds of administrative and managerial workers. Accordingly, all the sociologist can do is to use the available data as far as they can be used, and not be scared of using them where in his judgment they can yield tolerably valuable results merely because there are a number of cases in which they can tell him almost nothing.

Index

Ability, thwarting of 127
Abstract human labour 16, 34, 38
Accountants 34, 39, 66, 94, 121,
    129, 132, 164
Actors 164
Administration, public 49, 51, 59,
    71, 72, 93, 95, 98, 110, 120,
    132, 137, 141 f., 150, 164,
    165
    professional workers in 141 ff.
Administrative employees 11, 46,
    48, 99, 129, 165, 184
Adult education 5, 52, 96, 143
Agricultural employment in 1851,
    49
    workers 21, 46, 56, 74, 153
Agriculture, collectivization of 16,
    22
    concentration in 13, 92
Apprentices, premium 112
Apprenticeship 5, 53, 107, 108,
    112, 142, 150, 182, 183
Architects 67, 113, 129, 133, 137,
    164
Aristocracies, hereditary 37, 61,
    68 f., 82 ff., 91, 92, 103 f., 107,
    119, 134 ff. *See also* Landlords
    merchant 83 f.
Aristocratic elements in modern
    societies 12, 95, 116
Army, Navy and Air Force
    Officers, in Parliament 135,
    137; status of 120, 150
Arnold, Thomas 109 f.
Artists, social position of 70, 150
Austen, Jane 62
Authors 150, 164

Bankers, social status of 61, 120,
    129, 165
Banking, growth of 32 f., 85

Baxter, Dudley 55 ff., 60
Bolsheviks 22
Bourgeoisie 10, 12 f., 48, 87, 186
    and middle classes 90 ff., 100
    petite 12, 14, 48, 87, 147, 186
British Institute of Public Opinion
    43, 79
Builders, small master 15, 172
Bureaucracy 93, 141, 143
Burnham, James 98 f., 104 f.
Burt, Cyril 57

Capitalism, contradictions of 23,
    24, 88, 90, 97
    development of 82 ff.
    financial 87 f.
    in Russia 42
    in U.K. 97 f.
    in U.S.A. 97
    merchant 92
Capitalist concentration 15, 86,
    122
Capitalists, industrial 83 ff., 105,
    119 f., 122 f., 136
Carlyle, Thomas 29
Carr Saunders, Sir Alexander 57
Cash nexus 29
Caste 9
Casual workers 57, 151
Catholic Church, Roman 104, 118,
    138
Census data on Classes, British 5,
    43 f., 50 f., 148 ff., 188
    'industrial' and 'occupational'
    classifications 168
Centralism, democratic 17
Chamberlain, Joseph 140
Charisma 146
Charity schools 107, 114
Chartism 125
Chemistry, development of 34

For Product Safety Concerns and Information please contact our EU
representative GPSR@taylorandfrancis.com
Taylor & Francis Verlag GmbH, Kaufingerstraße 24, 80331 München, Germany

www.ingramcontent.com/pod-product-compliance
Lightning Source LLC
Chambersburg PA
CBHW050710280326
41926CB00088B/2912